HASR STO

D1150797

Please return or renew this item  **East Sussex**
by the last date shown. You may County Council
return items to any East Sussex
Library. You may renew books
by telephone or the internet.

0345 60 80 195 for renewals
0345 60 80 196 for enquiries

Library and Information Services
eastsussex.gov.uk/libraries

03750539 - **ITEM**

THE BIG SOCIETY

The Anatomy of the New Politics

Jesse Norman

First published in Great Britain in 2010 by
The University of Buckingham Press
Yeomanry House
Hunter Street
Buckingham MK18 1EG

© Jesse Norman

The moral right of the author has been asserted.

A CIP catalogue record for this book is available at the British Library.

ISBN 978 0 956 3952 0 7

In memory of Tom Bingham

Twitter summary (max. 140 characters)

There isn't one. Read the book.

If you only have three minutes:

How the Big Society redefines the political centre ground
> *Introduction*

How boom times impoverished us—*before* the financial crash
> *Chapter 1*

Government: Napoleonic, managerial and Presbyterian
> *Chapter 2*

Rigor mortis economics: where it came from…
> *Chapter 3*

… and why it fails
> *Chapter 4*

How the art of politics supplanted the art of government
> *Chapter 5*

How Labour undermined the left
> *Chapter 5*

The basic philosophy of the Big Society
> *Chapter 6*

Happiness (theory) is overrated. We should focus on capability
> *Chapter 7*

Why high rewards often reduce, not improve, performance
> *Chapter 7*

Conservatives should robustly defend common law rights
> *Chapter 8*

The Battle of Trafalgar was won in 1688—and what that means
> *Chapter 9*

Why a conservative ethics is not a contradiction in terms
> *Chapter 10*

The real meaning of *The Spirit Level*
> *Chapter 11*

The social power of music, and other policy ideas
> *Chapter 12*

Why excessive pay is an issue for us all, and what to do about it
> *Afterword*

Contents

Introduction

Intellectuals may not command many divisions. But they draw the maps by which the divisions march.

David Marquand

Conservative leader David Cameron first called for a "Big Society" in his Hugo Young lecture of November 2009:

The size, scope and role of government in Britain has reached a point where it is now inhibiting, not advancing, the progressive aims of reducing poverty, fighting inequality and increasing general well-being. Indeed there is a worrying paradox that because of its effect on personal and social responsibility, the recent growth of the state has promoted not social solidarity but selfishness and individualism.

But smaller government was not an automatic cure for social atomisation:

Instead, we need a thoughtful re-imagination of the role, as well as the size, of the state... actively helping to create the big society; directly agitating for, catalysing and galvanising social renewal.

Our alternative to big government is not no government— some reheated version of ideological laissez faire. Nor is it just smarter government. Our alternative to big government is the big society.

Social entrepreneurs and community activists already exist. But the big society also needs the engagement of that significant percentage of the population who have no record of getting involved—or desire to do so.

If we stick the course and change this country then we will have a national life expanded with meaning and mutual responsibility. We will feel it in the strength of our relationships—the civility and courtesy we show to each other.

Most political slogans have a life-cycle of days or hours. Yet it is already clear that the idea of the Big Society is taking root in the public mind.

But what exactly is the Big Society? What does it amount to? Is it "a return to a 19th century or US-style view of our welfare state" (Ed Miliband), "patronising nonsense" (Julia Goldsworthy) and "a big fat lie" (Polly Toynbee), or should we be offering two and a half cheers for it, with the Archbishop of Canterbury? Is it a mere PR slogan dreamed up to provide political cover for swingeing cuts to public services, or something more positive and profound? Is it hopelessly naïve in its expectations of society, or a realistic response to current social and economic problems?

These questions have been raised ever since the phrase was given public prominence during the Conservatives' 2010 General Election campaign. They have persisted, as the new Coalition government has placed the idea of the Big Society at the heart of their programme for government. Civil servants have sought for detail and definition. Satirists have fallen on the Big Society as the stuff of dreams, casting the Tories as do-gooding boy scouts determined to rescue society from its supposed moral failings, while perhaps disguising their own. And Labour have not been slow to reject the idea as a con, indeed a supposedly Thatcherite ruse to cut the state back to the bone and destroy the social fabric.

Meanwhile different commentators have been busily welcoming or disparaging the Big Society—sometimes both—according to their respective brands or preconceptions. A case in point is the widely respected *Guardian* columnist Jonathan Freedland, who used a July 2010 column to denounce the Coalition as a two-faced Janus with no clear narrative—rather than even consider the possibility that it could be acting in good conscience from a humane political viewpoint, albeit one which he did not appear to understand.

A week later he was back in print on the same subject. This time he conceded that "there's a good idea in Cameron's 'big society' screaming to get out", one which Labour would be ill-advised to oppose. Instead, he suggested, Labour politicians should mine their party's own traditions and co-opt the idea for themselves. That's a seven-day trajectory from denunciation to praise, whose total intellectual content amounts to the thought that the Big Society is a bad idea, or if it isn't then it's a Labour one. If this is its effect on someone as able as Jonathan Freedland, one might think, then the idea of a Big Society certainly needs urgent clarification.

Part of the problem is that we have lived for so long on a diet of top-down prescription and centralised government. This has bred the misconception that if there is not a clear centrally driven and centrally defined agenda, and a one-size-fits-all soundbite, then there is no policy. As a result politicians and pundits alike have simply rounded up the usual suspects.

But in so doing they have ignored what is actually happening. The Coalition government has not moved the Tories to the left or the LibDems to the right. It was created at the ballot box, and sealed with a referendum on the alternative vote. But it will be sustained by the Big Society; by a shared vision of social and economic renewal. Both parties are exploring an idea which cannot be understood using the conventional labels and political categories of left or right, which opens up hitherto unimagined areas of policy and debate, and which may amount to the most profound reshaping of the relationship between the individual and the state in modern times.

But that shared idea is also the glue that will hold the present government together. It is the new centre ground of British politics.

The Big Society

Moreover, little, if any, of the stock criticism is true. As this book will show, the Big Society is neither impossibly vague nor empty, either as an idea or as a political programme. It seeks to improve our public services, not undermine them. It is not ideologically opposed to the state, but deeply concerned—on the basis of overwhelming evidence—about the state's current ability to meet social needs and to support British society.

The Big Society is not, ultimately, a left- or right-wing idea as such. But crucially, it runs utterly counter to the state-first Fabianism of the modern Labour party. In the early 20th century the British left was a teeming mass of different intellectual and social traditions, encompassing guild socialism; religious nonconformism; civil dissent and suffragism; many shades of Marxism and Communism; mutuals and co-operatives; and unions. There was no necessity for this astonishing plurality to yield a political party which for fifty years has emphasised centralised state provision of public services above all else. No: this was the specific effect of the Fabians' takeover of Labour, as we shall see.

Thus the reason why the Big Society is so viscerally opposed by Labour politicians and their apologists is twofold. First, because it directly responds to huge public concern about the state of British society and the British economy; and second, because Labour itself is prevented in principle by its dominant Fabianism from drawing on the intellectual resources and traditions that would allow it to formulate a response. In the words of Simon Jenkins, Labour is trapped on Planet 1945. Co-option is not an option.

Or so I will argue. This book gathers together into a single narrative work done by the present author over the past five years, in particular *Compassionate Conservatism* (2006, with Janan Ganesh), *Compassionate Economics* (2008) and *Churchill's Legacy* (2009, with Peter Oborne). It derives from nearly three decades of reflection on these issues. The overall argument has been updated, deepened and developed into new areas. But it has not, and has not needed to be, significantly recast. Indeed a huge amount of new research work has emerged in recent years which confirms the overall analysis. Some of the many recent books which have echoed or extended this argument are listed in the End Notes.

Inevitably, this book discusses the present state of British politics, and offers some stringent criticism in places. But it is really about ideas and evidence, and only secondarily, if at all, about politics, politicians or ideology. It is addressed to those who are interested in political ideas and not political labels, be they of the left or right, who sense that there is something wrong in their lives at present, and who would like to do something about it. What it demands of the reader is a little time and a measure of fair-mindedness. What it offers is a new way of thinking about some old political problems.

What, then, is that argument? Essentially, it has two interlocking threads, which focus on the state and the individual. We start with the state. Is it working? Is it well-suited to the social and economic problems of the 21st century? Can it support us as a nation when we fall sick, when we are out of work or when we retire? Can it educate us and protect us properly? And if it can do so now, can it continue to do so in the future?

The growing evidence is that the state in its present form is manifestly insufficient to the task, in areas ranging from pensions to education, from housing to welfare provision. Indeed, we have reached the limits of the idea of the state as the remedy for social and economic failure. What is so striking is how impoverished political debate has become on these issues, and how reliant we are on a single and inflexible model of state provision of public services to solve our social ills. But if this is so, then the need to conceive an alternative approach is not optional for us; it is mandatory, indeed pressing. And it is mandatory not despite, but precisely because, our public services are so important, and because it is so important to enhance and develop them.

What we need, then, is a new vision of society: a humane, principled and long-term intellectual basis for our social renewal. This is not simply a matter of new policy or personnel. On the contrary, it requires the creation of a new political viewpoint: a rethinking of the basic categories of political debate and the nature of society from first principles, so as to be able to approach the whole spectrum of public issues and concerns anew, and in a fresh and intellectually authoritative way. At its heart, this book suggests, is the idea of what in 2006 I called a "connected society". This emphasises not the two-way opposition of state vs. individual, but the three-way relation of enabling state, active individual and linking institution.

One result of this shift in perspective is to render highly suspect much current political thinking. It reminds the political right to es-chew geographic metaphors; for what is really at stake is not static and quantitative, in the territory that is supposedly given up or gained by rolling back the state; but dynamic and qualitative, in improved social and economic well-being. But its real impact falls on the political left, whose continued equation of the interests of the state and of society has proven to be a catastrophic intellectual mistake. Indeed, it is not too much to say that while Labour remains in the grip of this Fabian error, its present lack of ideas and direction is not merely a short-lived accident, but the inescapable consequence of its basic assumptions. The greatest mistake Ed Miliband could make would be to ignore this gaping intellectual void and assume that current politics is just business as usual.

Politicians are generally very nervous about talking about ideas: in the words of the late, great Ernie Bevin, "open up that there Pandora's box, and who knows what Trojan Horses won't jump out of it". But of course to dismiss ideas is itself to be ruled by an idea. Ideas are al-ways in charge. In particular, we have well-developed theories of state action in politics, diplomacy, game theory and economics. We have well-developed theories of individual action in ethics and psychology. What we lack are well-developed theories with which to understand and explain the behaviour of institutions.

We know enough already, however, to be able to make a bold conjecture with some confidence. This is that even a slow transformation of this country into a more connected society would release staggering amounts of social energy and capital. This energy lies shackled beneath the surface of British society at present; held back by deference, class division, regulation, poverty, foolish theory and lack of political imagination. It is time to power it up and set it free.

Rigor Mortis Economics

Thus the Big Society, as conceived here, is not a mere political slogan. It is a so far largely instinctual attempt to tap into and release this latent social energy. Its intellectual counterpart must be a thoroughgoing attempt to think through the ideas of a free society and of free institutions—to provide an anatomy of the new politics.

To do that, we do not simply need a better vision of society; we need a better understanding of the individual, of what it is to be human. Our view has become distorted by a received textbook idea of economics, which has distorted public policy and undermined our cultural identity.

In particular, far more needs to be said about our basic assumptions as to economics itself. British government and the general public have become far more knowledgeable about economics since the 1970s. But they have grown up with a standard 1970s school-book caricature of what economics is, and of economic man as perfectly rational and self-interested. Keynes's famous dictum that "practical men ... are usually the slaves of some defunct economist" has applied with a vengeance. Except in this case it is not one economist as such but a whole standard economic model that has enslaved them, and us.

This *rigor mortis* economics has had two disastrous effects. The first is political: it has massively reinforced a thirty-year trend to greater centralisation and micro-management within government. Under Labour large parts of Whitehall, and in particular the Treasury, have fallen into a narrow and technocratic view of society. The result has been an extension of the tax and benefits system to include nearly 70% of the adult population of this country; an obsession with setting and monitoring performance targets; and endless fiddling with programmes in response to new initiatives or political wheezes. Within the public sector as a whole, it has helped to create a culture of low innovation and low productivity.

Typically, a particular group of people will be identified as in need of a state "intervention". The group will be specified mathematically and modelled financially in terms of its income or assets. Finally, the economic incentives it faces will be tweaked by the Treasury through the tax and/or benefits systems, or through other public spending decisions.

This dismal economic gospel regards the human world as static, not dynamic: as a world of fixed social engineering, not one of creation, discovery and competition. It is doing huge damage to our economy and our society. Intellectually, as we shall show, it cannot be right. Yet it has its advocates. They can defend themselves by pointing at their mathematical models and asking, properly, for flaws in the reasoning. Until critics can explain what has gone wrong here, and why and how economics itself must be re-embedded within a wider social and cultural debate, they will lack the theoretical resources to implement an alternative political vision.

But the argument is also about us, about our culture and iden-tity—the other side of the Big Society. If the received understanding of economics within government is radically incomplete, how much more so is it within society as a whole. We have been brought up and are daily conditioned to think of human beings as the "agents" of textbook economics: as purely self-interested, endlessly calculating costs and benefits, and highly sensitised to marginal gains and losses. And part of the achievement of economists since Adam Smith is to explain to us why this is OK—how individual self-interest can become social well-being.

But a problem comes when this economic image feeds back and becomes our default picture of human motivation. For we secretly know this picture is wrong. We know that it coarsens our public life, undermines trust and degrades our civic expectations. We know that there are routine aspects of our daily lives like volunteering or philanthropy which it cannot properly explain. We know that there are virtues such as loyalty and long-term thinking which seem to run directly counter to it.

The result is that we fret about the atomisation of society, the commercialisation of human culture and the narrowing of our ex-pectations of others. We over-invest in half-baked prescriptions for happiness. We yearn endlessly for the things money famously cannot buy: love, friendship, joy. Yet without an alternative picture of what a human being is, we cannot free ourselves from our assumptions. This is the intellectual counterpart of reflection about a free society and free institutions.

Instead we need to take the idea of human capability far more seriously. Independent institutions and individuals have capabili-ties—such as to govern, to bring people together, to play, to learn, to act, to think. Capabilities require freedom to develop, and a measure of risk. They can be exercised well or badly, wisely or foolishly, virtuously or corruptly. They both live off and fuel a culture of openness, entrepreneurship and dissent. Indeed, some notion of capability is positively required to discharge the idea of responsibility on which David Cameron has placed so much public emphasis.

Essentially, books about political issues fall into two groups. The first chart the ebb and flow of political fortunes, the frothy surface waves of who said what to whom, who's up or down, in or out. They are novelistic, personal and rooted in the present. Their interest, if any, lies in revelation and drama. The second group chart the deeper currents. They look less at personalities and more at ideas and governing assumptions. They take a long-run view. Their interest, if any, lies in the quality of their analysis, explanation and prediction.

This book falls into the latter category. It explains how an ancient theory of human flourishing can be used to develop a far richer conception of human character and well-being. And it shows how that concept can be used to guide public policy today, in the Britain of the 21st century. *It doesn't have to be this way; we could be doing so much better.*

Thus Chapters 1-3 examine the sources of our political, economic and social weakness—the state we're really in. Chapters 4-7 then dig down to bedrock, and look at the basic assumptions of economics and politics that condition our current thinking. Those assumptions are crucially flawed. But correcting them clears the way for a deep explanation of the Big Society and its radically different view of human nature.

Chapters 8 and 9 explore two key areas where the Big Society has important implications—the rule of law and economic renewal—

while Chapter 10 shows how the idea dovetails with David Cameron's new compassionate conservatism. Chapter 11 develops the Big Society as a political programme, and answers its critics. The book closes with some final and perhaps unexpected policy conclusions.

1 The British Economy: Mirage or Miracle?

> We cannot solve problems with the same kind
> of thinking we used to create them.
> *Albert Einstein*

When asked in 1997 how the new Labour government was to be judged on the key issue of equality, Peter Mandelson would only say, in his characteristically grand and self-confident way: "Judge us after ten years of success in office. For one of the fruits of that success will be that Britain has become a more equal society."

That moment came slightly late, in June 2009, with the publication of *Towards a More Equal Society?*, a comprehensive analysis of Labour's first decade produced by the left-leaning London School of Economics and the Joseph Rowntree Foundation. The LSE's boffins were meticulous, thorough and wide-ranging. Their summary was a masterpiece of even-handedness. It is an, ah, mixed picture. It all depends on what you look at, and when. More work is undoubtedly needed.

So let us decode. Beneath its measured exterior the book is a screaming howl of pain at the way a Labour—Labour!—government blew the opportunity of a lifetime to make real inroads into inequality.

There were wins, of course: child and pensioner poverty were down, the poorest children were doing better in school, and there had been gains in tackling deprivation.

But health inequalities had widened. The UK was still bottom of the EU15 countries in child poverty. Many changes to taxation under Labour had been regressive, hitting the poor relatively more than the rich. There were 900,000 more people in severe poverty than in 1997, while the gap in life expectancy between rich and poor now was at its widest since the Victorian era. Note too that these findings predated the present economic recession, with all its malign expected social effects.

What is so tragic is that after 1997 the conditions for a concerted attack on inequality were just about perfect. The Blair government had political momentum, there was a widely held belief across British society that money needed to be spent on public services, and the public coffers were filling fast. Indeed we can go further: the UK economy after 1997, while very far from perfect, may well have been in its best condition since the Second World War. Gone were the foreign exchange crises of the 1940s-1970s. Gone was the struggle to take control of monetary policy of the 1980s and early 1990s.

Now, as the LSE's analysis shows, all that is history. During the past thirteen years more than a trillion—a thousand billion—extra pounds have been spent over the levels inherited in 1997. Yet the economy is struggling, public attitudes towards redistribution are hardening, and our rapidly ageing population will lock the door on public spending on anything like the scale seen under Blair and Brown. It will not recur for a generation. New thinking is called for, on a gigantic scale.

That thinking is what inspires the Big Society. But first we need to look at a basic issue more deeply. Despite what many commentators have said, that issue is not the financial crash and its aftermath. It lies in the fundamental direction of British economic and social policy. That is the paradigm, and we need to break out of it.

The Conventional Wisdom

We start with the economy. Until 2008, the conventional wisdom about Great Britain was this: the British economy of the past two decades has been a huge success story. Gone were the days of boom and bust, as the country enjoyed continuous economic growth since its exit from the European Exchange Rate Mechanism in 1992. Sure, there were occasional crises: there was the Asia crisis, the Russia crisis, the end of the dot-com boom, the terrorist attacks of 9/11, and the Iraq war. All of these were serious events, with serious consequences for the world economy. Yet although Britain was clearly affected by them, they could not stop or reverse its economic growth. That record of economic expansion stretched over more than 60 consecutive quarters.

However, the story runs on, it was not only Britain's economic growth that was remarkable. Interest rates, which had been in the double digits only 15 years ago, fell in the mid-1990s and then stayed for over a decade at historically low levels. Inflation, which had been all but impossible to control for much of the 1970s and 1980s, turned into virtual price stability. Unemployment, the bane of Britain for much of her post-war history, was replaced by near-full employment.

Finally, the conventional wisdom continues, there was internal change. The structure of Britain's economy shifted dramatically away from manufacturing and towards services. Unproductive and unprofitable "sunset" industries declined, while new clean, creative and international "sunrise" businesses grew rapidly. Financial services in particular grew to become Britain's most important success story, with the City of London arguably the world's most successful financial hub. With all this spectacular transformation, Britain could claim to be one of the very first post-modern economies, ahead of her Continental European neighbours and competitors.

This picture had an interesting asymmetry. When the British economy was riding high, the reason was said to be Mr Brown's far-sighted economic management. When it started to struggle, however, the rhetoric became that this was due to forces outside the then-government's control. There was a collapse of the US sub-prime lending market, rising oil and food prices, and a crisis in domestic and international financial institutions. If the British economy finally succumbed to recession, well, that was only to be expected in the face of global economic forces.

So much for the conventional wisdom. Some of it is true. But the bigger picture is far more interesting, and far more problematic. The British economy has done much less well in recent years than is normally understood. The specific reason why this country has endured the longest and deepest recession on record is that it was grossly over-extended and unprepared for the financial crash when it came. That lack of preparedness had little if anything to do with the US sub-prime market. On the contrary, it derived from a succession of booms in different UK markets which the then government was unable to identify or unwilling to restrain. In other words, one of the negative effects of the crash has been to obscure an accurate understanding of the underlying state of the UK economy, and how it came to be that way.

We can recover some of that understanding by considering the UK economy up to 2008, when the crash occurred. As we shall see, the fundamental drivers of our long-term prosperity have become relatively weaker, not stronger, over the past decade. And a key part of the reason for that has been that British government has placed too much faith in a relatively unproductive and constricting state.

Treading Water

To return: contrary to the conventional wisdom, Britain's economic performance since 1993 has flattered to deceive, in two ways. The first lies in the contrast with Britain's post-war economic decline. By the 1970s the country had fallen far behind its major competitors, after three decades of relative economic decline. So the change from struggling economy to economic leader in the 1990s looked spectacular.

But we must also note the contrast with Britain's international competitors today. Of course Britain is more prosperous than it was twenty, thirty or forty years ago; so is every other major industrial economy. The real question is how Britain has done in relative terms. When British politicians celebrate the country's growth record, they usually compare it with those of the big economies of the Eurozone, Germany, France and Italy. And indeed the UK significantly outperformed those countries in GDP growth after 1992, the final year of the last UK recession. Until the recession of 2008 took hold, the UK economy had grown by about 50% since then in real terms, while the economic growth of the Eurozone was less than 40%.

Not bad, one might say. But look again. For one thing, the Eurozone's growth was held back by Germany, its industrial engine, which went through a painful and expensive process of re-unification. But the real point is that the major Euro economies are quite unlike that of the UK, with highly regulated labour markets, and a much greater emphasis on manufacturing than services. For similar reasons, though there is every reason for UK policymakers to be nervous about the extraordinary growth and economic ambition of China, India or Brazil, it makes little sense to compare our economy directly with theirs.

No, the real comparison should be with countries with a similar cultural, political and economic background to this one, in particular the principal mature free-market economies in the OECD whose language is English: Australia, Canada, the United States, New Zealand and Ireland. **And every single one of these countries grew faster over the period 1992-2008 than Britain**. Canada grew by 59% in economic terms, the United States by 60%, New Zealand by 62% and Australia by 73%. Ireland's position is deceptive since it had some catching up to do, but its growth record of 167% between 1992 and 2006 was over three times that of the UK.

So the true picture looks like this: the UK economy grew faster since 1992 than the sluggish economies of Europe. But it lagged behind those of other more genuinely comparable industrial nations. Our growth was remarkable only for its mediocrity. Instead of an economic miracle, we were treading water at best.

Unfortunately even this picture is too rosy. You can have national economic growth with no genuine improvement if it is just a result of more people working. Imagine an economy which doubled its GDP by employing twice the number of people: its GDP per capita would remain unchanged. The wealth of the average individual would remain exactly the same, and any talk of real economic growth would miss the point.

Something similar happened to Britain over the period under review. While the economy grew by around 50%, much of this growth simply occurred because there was an influx of people who enlarged the workforce, and of course also became consumers. An extra three million people found employment in Britain—roughly 10% of the total workforce. Once they are factored in, it turns out that UK GDP per head in fact only improved by 42% between 1992 and 2008. In other words, the UK's growth record was even weaker than appeared at first sight, and only just above the growth figures of the "sclerotic" Eurozone. Our "economic miracle" was a mirage.

Four Booms

Economic growth is not everything, of course, even to economists. It also matters, for example, how it is achieved. How has the UK's economic growth over the past 10-15 years been achieved?

Again, the answer is not encouraging from a long-term economic perspective. As many people are now coming to understand, the UK economy was sustained by four booms over the decade after 1997: in government spending, in immigration, in house price inflation and in personal debt.

By way of backdrop, we need to recall that the period 1997-2007 was what Mervyn King, the Governor of the Bank of England, called the NICE—Non-Inflationary Consistent Expansion—decade. Worldwide monetary conditions were extremely favourable, with interest rates and headline inflation in the major industrial countries generally at post-war lows. The low cost of borrowing was the crucial backdrop to these four booms, for when money is cheap it is easy for individuals, and governments, to borrow.

Thus the first boom—the massive ramp up in public spending after 2001—was financed not only by taxation, but by a large and countercyclical increase in government debt. Under normal circumstances the conventional wisdom is that the public finances should record a slight surplus in boom times to balance out the inevitable annual deficits when the economy slows down. There was a surplus between 1999 and 2002, but after that the government ran a deficit, even without including the effect of rapidly escalating off-balance sheet liabilities such as public sector pensions and Private Finance Initiative (PFI) debt. According to the OECD, by 2007 the UK had the largest structural budget deficit in the G7. Indeed, the UK had a budget deficit of 3% of GDP at a time when the economy was still growing at nearly 3% a year: a clear sign that the country's finances were not in balance. Since the financial crisis and the government's bail-out of the banks, of course, the budget deficit has grown yet more massively to £159 billion, or 11% of GDP in 2010—the highest in the G20.

The growth in government spending helped to ramp up domestic demand and economic activity. And the economy was further supported by a second boom, in immigration. This escalated quickly after 1997. But when the UK opened its labour market to workers from Poland and other East European countries in 2004, it offered an unmissable opportunity. The Polish zloty was weak against the pound, while wages in Britain were on average seven times higher than in Poland. The Poles were well educated. Many spoke English and there was a large young population of skilled workers willing to relocate. An estimated 500,000 came to the UK. As well as pushing up GDP they added to domestic demand, while their relatively low pay helped to keep down reported inflation.

However, the boom in immigration was dwarfed by a third boom, in housing. Housing is the only area of the UK economy in which price inflation is widely welcomed—but only, of course, by those already on the housing ladder. The fundamentals of the UK housing market encourage this inflationary trend: in particular the lack of land supply, due in part to strict planning controls and a system of local government finance which discourages local development. Taken with significant population growth, low interest rates and an explosion in credit, the effect between 1992 and 2007 was to push house prices up to astronomical levels. House prices more than doubled in real terms over this period. Excessive mortgages of 100-125% of value became commonplace. Banks were only too willing to lend people five or six times their salaries; and even more if they were prepared to "self-certify" their own financial circumstances.

House price inflation soon became a self-fulfilling prophecy, and over time the UK economy increasingly came to be built around it. One crucial effect of this was to erode further the nation's already-weakening desire to save. In the early 1990s UK households still saved about 8% of their disposable net income. They saved for all the reasons that people usually put money aside: to pay for a new car, to spend it on a future holiday, to have a better life in retirement, or simply to have some reserves for a rainy day. This positive trend changed in 2004. After that UK households have had negative net savings rates until the recession hit.

Many things undermined the British desire to save, including the dot-com boom and bust and a series of stock market and insurance scandals. But the most influential by far was the impact of apparently ever-rising house prices. Putting your money in the bank seemed less and less attractive to many people as house prices soared. Why get 2% or 3% a year on your savings account when you could get 7% or 8% in the housing market, and more if you leveraged up and took on extra debt? Thus did the housing bubble become further inflated.

But many prospective buyers also felt they had little choice. As houses became more expensive, they had to stretch still more financially just to be able to afford a decent place to live, and this squeezed out saving still further.

The rise in asset values in turn fuelled a fourth boom, in personal debt. Historically, consumption rested on thrift: you had to save up over time in order to buy a car or a kitchen or a foreign holiday. But for many people in the 2000s, rising property prices seemed to make this kind of saving a thing of the past. Wasn't it much easier to borrow against the value of your house in the hope, nay expectation, of a further rise in house prices?

In this way some £250 billion was withdrawn from the property market. Much of it, together with a huge amount of new unsecured lending, went straight into consumption. The UK became a nation of consumers who were more than happy to gamble in the property market and buy plasma TVs on credit. Personal debt soared to nearly £1.5 trillion. Average household indebtedness more than doubled between 1997 and 2007 from £24,650 to £56,501. Where only twenty years earlier personal debt had stood at below 60% of GDP, in 2007 it was, for the first time in history, higher than Britain's entire annual economic output. Eighty per cent of that debt was secured on private property. Thus the credit crunch, when it came, fell upon an economy that was already hugely indebted and overstretched.

Ignoring the Fundamentals

Britain has not, then, experienced an economic "miracle" since 1997, or even 1992. The economy has been sustained by easy global monetary conditions, by cheap credit at home, and by four huge economic stimuli in particular. Far from abolishing the normal cycle of boom and bust, the last Labour government presided over a huge expansion in demand which served only to defer economic reality, to postpone the need for adjustments, and to worsen the eventual reckoning. When that reckoning came, when reality broke in and the financial crisis struck, the effects were correspondingly worse because the UK's economy was already so over-extended, and its public finances so vulnerable. The effect was to make the resultant UK recession the longest and deepest of any major industrialised country. This is Mr Brown's legacy as Chancellor and Prime Minister. His record cannot be defended by pointing out that the financial crisis started in the USA, since the claim does not concern the origins of the crisis, but its uniquely damaging effects on the UK.

Even so, we might be somewhat comforted if there were reason to think that the foundations of our economic prosperity—such as our national productivity, our institutional and legal framework, and above all our educational system—had been greatly strengthened. But here again there is real cause for concern. The truth is that none of these four booms made much relative difference to the fundamental drivers of wealth creation in this country. Indeed, on the whole their effect may even have been to weaken those drivers.

There was, to put it mildly, no shortage of public spending over this period. For the total increase—note, increase—in government expenditure over 1997 levels in the period 1997-2008 was of the order of £1.2 trillion pounds. If this colossal sum had been used in part to provide the UK with a world-class education system or a world-class transport infrastructure, that would be one thing. If our rates of innovation and productivity had significantly risen during this period, that would be another. If there had been a shift towards a more balanced and long-term-oriented economy, that would be a third. But they have not. We are still discussing the same problems today that we were ten years ago. The structural weaknesses of the UK economy have remained. And it is only just starting to sink in that the most fundamental problems of our economy, and our society, cannot be solved by more money alone.

A similar story can be told across the public sector. Take the education system, which on any reckoning is vital to our long-term economic and social well-being. It alone has seen ever-greater central control of the curriculum; a huge increase in testing; and the proliferation of new quangos. Each of these has its own remit, staff, CEO and board and funding; each seeks to justify itself through endless activity of often dubious value, often overlapping with and contradicting the others—and while a proliferation of new private companies tends to create competition, the trend in the public sector is for new organisations to cross-refer to each other, with further paperwork and loss of productivity. Public spending on education rose by £38 billion a year—thirty-eight billion pounds a year—in the decade after 1997.

And to what result? The quality of school education in the UK appears to have fallen, not risen, compared to other countries. We have slipped far down the international league tables in education. For example, the OECD's benchmark Programme for International Student Assessment study found that the UK ranked 24th among 57 nations for maths, and 17th for literacy. In 2000, it was eighth in maths and seventh in literacy respectively. Another fundamental driver of our prosperity has been seriously weakened.

Moreover, our four booms have been episodic in character. They have washed through the British economy with relatively little positive legacy. We have already seen their disastrous effects on personal debt and on our savings habits. But consider immigration, which is often considered a great economic success story, again. Many people now have new kitchens and house extensions as a result of imported labour. Yet there is also reason to believe it has encouraged a long-term de-skilling of British workers in manual trades, who have been squeezed out by the temporary competition from abroad. It is notable that a bipartisan House of Lords report found "no evidence … of significant economic benefits" from recent immigration. Meanwhile, the warm glow of apparent economic success served to disguise the fact that the UK has almost certainly become less economically competitive over the past decade. A recent World Bank study placed the UK top as a place to do business in only one category—ease of obtaining credit.

But, one might ask, how can this be? How can 15 years of prosperity have failed to make us more competitive or resilient? How can government have spent so much and saved so little? Why did it fail to take the extraordinary opportunity after 1997 to address our deep social and economic problems?

There are many reasons. However, the elephant in the room is the huge growth of the state, and its accompanying ideology of centralisation, managerialism and intervention. As we shall see in due course, the Big Society stands as a thorough repudiation and corrective to that ideology. But first we need to look at the history and working of the state itself. This is the subject of the next chapter.

2 **The State We're Really In**

> The economic crisis should have been (and indeed still can be) the moment when, instead of lazily succumbing to the idea that more state spending dressed up as fiscal stimulus is the sole answer, we took the opportunity to accelerate and sharpen reform.
>
> *Tony Blair,* A Journey

Political traditions wax and wane. But one crucial continuity has been the steady growth, in some form or other, of "the state" in this country over the last nine hundred years. However, it is only after 1945 that the state has assumed its recognisable modern form. Since then, we can identify four broad phases in its development: enlargement in the late 1940s and 1950s, stasis in the 1960s and 1970s, selective retrenchment in the 1980s, and further extension after 1997.

Over this period all the main political parties have, with one partial exception, accepted this continuing pattern of state growth. They have done so from a belief that a large state was a guarantor of good public services and social well-being. This view has become progressively more untenable, as we shall see. And it has in turn encouraged politicians, officials and people to identify state and society altogether—to see them as one and the same. Independent institutions, the heart of the Big Society, have been largely pushed to the margins.

The exception is, of course, Mrs Thatcher. It is hard to fathom now how lacking British citizens were in 1979 in the basic economic freedoms that we now take for granted. Huge parts of the UK economy were directly owned by the state, including all or part of the telecoms, water, electricity, coal, steel, shipbuilding, road and air transport and car industries. Wages were restrained by collective agreement between government and the unions, and labour markets were rigid and im-mobile. The prices of many goods were determined by government fiat, not by market mechanisms. Foreign exchange controls strictly limited the amounts of money that could be brought in or out of the country, and so restricted foreign direct investment. The top rate of income tax was 83%.

This relative economic decline could not continue, and it did not. In response, Mrs Thatcher rolled back the frontiers of the state. She abolished exchange controls, cut direct taxation, deregulated the City of London in the "Big Bang", broke the power of the unions and freed up labour markets. Her government privatised half of what was known as the "State Trading Sector", and sold off a quarter of the stock of council housing.

But less famously, the Thatcher government also greatly central-ised what remained. The deep issue behind the economic decline of the 1970s had been the increasing ungovernability of Great Britain. This showed itself in, among other things, a lack of control over public expenditure. In particular, the rise in spending towards 50% of GDP in 1975-76 precipitated a fiscal crisis and forced the Callaghan government to call in the IMF. Throughout the 1980s Whitehall was desperately seeking to restrain public spending and inflation, and this, plus the increasing demand for central accountability for spending, fed through into greater central control in education, health and policing. The effect was most felt in local government where many local councils spent heavily and raised their rates (and so inflation, since rates were included in inflation calculations), in part for hostile political reasons. In reaction, the Thatcher government imposed central regulation of local spending, pulled more tax powers back to the centre, and capped local rates.

As this potted history brings out, there are two ways in which the state can grow. It can grow economically, quantitatively, in pounds, shillings and pence by taking more of what we produce in taxes every year. Or it can grow socially, qualitatively, in the different ways in which it affects our lives, our goals and projects. A new regulation may have no effect on GDP, but a huge effect on how we live. The state can be extensive, or it can be pervasive, or both.

The Thatcher government reduced the pervasiveness of the state, in ways we have seen. But economically, its extent was almost unchanged between 1979 and 1997, at about 36%-37% of GDP consumed in taxes. Since 1997, however, the state has grown fast in both directions. Before the financial crisis it was projected to cost 43% of GDP in taxes in 2010, a rise of about one-fifth in 13 years. This would be bad enough; but the actual outcome has been that the state now consumes a staggering 48%, more than ten full percentage points over 1997. Meanwhile the number of those directly or indirectly employed by the state rose during Labour's first decade to 6.8 million, or 784,000 more than in 1997.

But it is on the harder-to-measure social, qualitative side that the difference is most marked. Tony Blair's second and third term took some measures to decentralise power, in particular via its Foundation Trust and Academies programmes. It talked endlessly about community empowerment and citizenship, and launched a series of Commissions and Action Plans. But the reality was that these plans emphasised participation rather than content, reflecting an official, process-driven view of social interaction rather than a substantive one. In many cases "community fundraising" came to mean simply fundraising from different state bodies, rather than actually putting a philanthropic idea to the test with local people. The result has been eloquently described as "faking civil society", and created further reliance on the state.

The overall trend under Labour was towards centralisation, however, with the state becoming hugely more pervasive after 1997. For example: its Tax Credits did not merely means-test household income, but demanded details of household costs in order to pay for people's childcare. Its Pension Credit was introduced to help poor pensioners, but is projected to provide state financial support to 75% of all pensioners by 2050 as a result of the rapid growth of means-testing. Its Child Trust Funds or "baby bonds" introduced the state into people's lives at birth, while the Sure Start programme extended the state's influence during early years.

Outside the Ministries themselves, a huge quangocracy of unelected bodies arose to exercise public power on behalf of ministers, but with minimal accountability to Parliament. In August 2007 it was revealed that government spending on quangos had risen by 700% since 1998. To take one notorious example, before its abolition the Learning and Skills Council—an organization whose purpose was merely to allocate funding to vocational education institutions—had 148 people in its Human Resources department alone. After its abolition, five new quangos took its place.

Meanwhile foolish or unnecessary regulation proliferated under Labour. International surveys show that the legal burden of doing business in Britain significantly increased. Thus Tolley's tax manuals, the industry standard reference work, increased in length from 2,529 pages in 1997 to 7,838 pages in 2008. Vast amounts of new legislation were introduced—much of it deriving from EU directives—in such areas as health and safety, employment law and planning, as well as within specific industries. Huge and costly new industries of compliance and audit duly arose to monitor and enforce that legislation.

So why, then, did this occur? It bears restating that this new statism is not an accident. On the contrary, its causes are deeply ideological. In the words of Professor Anthony Giddens, the supposed guru of the Third Way, "Only a welfare system that benefits most of the population will generate a common morality of citizenship." This extraordinary statement rests on so many false and socially malign assumptions as to defy brief analysis. It implies a deliberate attempt to engineer the widest possible dependence of British citizens on the state. Formally, the language of state socialism has been abandoned. But in actual fact a new level of intervention has been added.

Thus under Gordon Brown, the state did not merely carry on its traditional functions of taxation, policing and defence, or the post-1945 functions of the welfare state, or the commitment to active labour and industrial policies of earlier Labour governments. On the contrary it, and specifically Whitehall, developed a direct relationship with all British citizens and residents. Almost all contributed to taxation, and a majority received some form of financial support rationed according to need; either by means testing, or via ad hoc transfers, such as the Winter Fuel Payment and the Council Tax Rebate. In the name of efficiency, there was a minimum of independent hierarchy or other intervening institutions between the Treasury and the home. The ethos of government became one of continuous intervention and micro-management, in which specific groups were targeted and economic incentives tweaked in order to redistribute resources or change behaviour—with huge complexity and fraud in the tax and benefit systems as a result. Standing in the centre over the past decade, mediating these transfers, and assessing merit or worth, has been central government.

This view owes much to the Scottish Kirk, a church in which similar themes of absence of hierarchy, individual worth and salvation, all-inclusive community and a direct relationship with God are to be found. And there is a further important shared theme: a commitment to moralising. The central focus of a Kirk service is normally on preaching; on the transmission of Presbyterian principles ultimately based on the Westminster Confession of Faith of 1647. Similarly, the Brownian state was not merely a vehicle with the power to do good, and motivated by a political desire to do so. It was designed to be a channel for the transmission of certain values throughout society, as though a sense of community could only be achieved through shared dependence on the state. This is the early import of Professor Giddens's words.

But we should not expect the state under Blair and Brown to have been shaped by a single vision. In fact under Labour there were two other themes, both led by Tony Blair. One was that of *dirigisme* or central direction in the French style. Tony Blair came to power promising to lead a "Napoleonic" government, and this he achieved. The role and responsibilities of the cabinet were much diminished. A new cadre of special advisers was hired alongside career civil servants. The centre exercised much tighter control over departmental spending, over dealings with the press and "news management", and over appointments. Parliament was treated by ministers, and by the Prime Minister, with disdain.

The other theme was a corporate one: Labour saw the state as in effect a national corporation, with the Prime Minister as Chief Executive and the Chancellor as Chief Financial Officer. Historically, the proper constitutional role of the Prime Minister has been that of first among equals in the cabinet. But over a generation this morphed into a role as CEO: as both the principal commissioner of policy change and its main political manager. New legislation, no matter how ill-considered or foolish, was equated with corporate turnover. As a result, the number of new laws was 1,724 a year on average during the 1980s, but 3,071 a year on average under Blair and Brown.

The influence of the corporate model on Labour was manifest both in language and in action, in such things as "UK PLC"; the Prime Minister's "Delivery Unit", the central office charged with ensuring that No. 10's plans were achieved; the proliferation of public service targets, supported by opaque management speak; its huge over-reliance on off-balance-sheet financing, whose true cost was often unclear; a growing view among politicians that civil servants were the economic agents or employees of the government, rather than servants of the Crown; the vast extension of Prime Ministerial patronage; the relegation of government departments from being semi-autonomous entities towards a new status as divisions of the whole; a view of citizens as "clients" or "customers"; a view of personal incentives as purely a matter of carrot and stick; and the increasing informality and absence of procedure at the top of government. Some of these trends existed before 1997. Some existed before 1979. But all were greatly accelerated under Labour.

The Problem of Productivity

Some of these developments are to be welcomed. But many will regard them with unease, whatever their own political affiliations. Those on the right may feel a natural instinct to rein back what they see as the fell hand of government. Those on the left, even if they regard the state as generally beneficent, may nonetheless feel concern at its impact on individual liberties.

The key issues here are not ideological, however, but practical. They assume, rather than questioning, the vital importance of having good public services in this country, of high quality and open to all. They are about means, not ends. Is this new statism working? Is it well-suited to the social and economic problems of the 21st century?

The clear evidence is that it is not. On the contrary, the inefficiency of the state is undermining our long-term growth and productivity. Tax-financed expenditures have been estimated to have a negative economic impact on real GDP growth of between 0.14% and 0.25% for every percentage point rise, each year. Even the lower figure would imply a total drag on growth of just over 1% a year from the increased size of the public spending burden between 1997 and 2010.

But an even deeper problem concerns productivity. Productivity is an abstract concept, which is notoriously subject to change and hard to measure. The term broadly refers to our ability to generate goods and services more efficiently over time: to get more output from a given input. It is thus a basic driver of a country's long-term prosperity.

The UK is often thought to be similar in its cultural and economic expectations to the US. But as regards productivity, the difference is marked. The US has gone through a productivity revolution in recent years, a step-change in its underlying ability to produce goods and

nd the trend in US productivity growth, having moved up a
he 1990s, accelerated after that. Experts differ as to precisely
what has happened and why. But the main reason seems to lie in the
interaction between two things: first, the traditional advantages the
US offers to business such as flexible labour markets, relatively low
taxation and low regulation; and secondly, the degree to which its
companies have pushed the new telecoms and information technologies into their businesses, especially in manufacturing and retailing.

The UK has seen almost all the same technologies over this period,
and in areas such as telecoms it has even been ahead of the US. Yet
it has not seen a step-change in productivity. On the contrary, its
performance has steadily weakened over the past ten years. Nor is UK
productivity growth accelerating. Quite the opposite: it is growing
more slowly than in the past, more slowly than in our main industrialised competitors in North America and the EU and in Japan, and far
more slowly than in China and India.

Moreover, UK productivity is specifically being pulled down by
the performance of the state sector. Notably, a joint report by the
Treasury and Downing Street Strategy Unit found that public sector
productivity fell by 10 per cent between 1997 and 2003. The first
year of Gordon Brown's premiership saw a spurt in public spending in 2008-9 in an effort to boost productivity. But a 2010 ONS
report showed that the actual result was not a rise but a sharp fall in
productivity. There were specific falls in adult social care, education,
healthcare, public order and safety, and children's social care.

What of existing public services, though? What is the impact of
slowing productivity on them? Take the NHS. Funding has more
than doubled in cash terms since 1997. Of course, some of this
money has gone into improving services and health outcomes. But

it has also meant that NHS costs have risen fast, as much as twice the national inflation rate for much of the 2000s. But NHS productivity growth has, even on the most favourable estimate, been just 1% p.a. since 1999.

The NHS is in an extraordinarily difficult position. It is a near-monopoly provider operating in a market of escalating service expectations, with which successive governments have continuously interfered, and to which the British public is deeply attached. In the longer term, however, what are the alternatives for the NHS in its present form? There are only two. Either it consumes more and more public spending, crowding out other important public priorities; or it grows its spending at the long term growth rate of the economy and does progressively less with what spending it has.

The paradox is that the funding squeeze made necessary by the current financial crisis is likely to help curb the cost inflation that has beset the NHS in recent years. But the effects of this high inflation have long been apparent. Costly new drugs with proven therapeutic effects were rationed or withheld. Many patient preferences, such as the preference among many diabetics for inhaled over injected insulin, were set aside. Premature babies, who could go on to live happy and worthwhile lives, were described by one of the Royal Colleges of Medicine even in 2006 as "bed-blockers" impeding the treatment of other babies, such was the pressure on resources. The NHS increasingly looks at "lifestyle" factors such as obesity and smoking in deciding whether a given treatment is available. These trends can only continue.

Similar patterns can be seen in other areas of public services and welfare, in housing and in education. The conclusion must be that it is less and less credible that the state alone can continue to fund and plan not merely the new public services of the future, but even our present public services as they stand. New models, new social resources and new energy—indeed a new conception of the relation between state and society itself—are called for.

Baumol's Cost Disease

Now it might be argued that these problems are relatively short-term, stable and circumstantial: merely teething problems, after which everything will settle down, and efficiency and productivity will return. In fact, however, these problems are long term, almost certain to increase, and intrinsic to the nature of public services.

To see why, we need to make a brief detour into the performing arts. In 1966 the economists William Baumol and William Bowen published a seminal article on productivity in the performing arts. The problem is this: imagine you are a member of a string quartet. Every year you and your colleagues need a pay-rise to keep pace with inflation. But your productivity hardly increases. You can't drop a member and still play the Hoffmeister quartet with three people, and when you do play it, it will still last about as long as it did when Mozart wrote it in 1786. If you worked in a car factory, on the other hand, there would be no problem: productivity has risen hugely in the car industry as a result of technology, automation and supply chain management. This generates gains, part of which can be passed on to employees. Costs go up but output, normally, goes up faster.

This phenomenon is known among economists as "Baumol's cost disease". It arises generally in service industries, which tend to be hard to automate, hard to standardise, and reliant on the personal touch. If you have ever wondered why new car costs are low while car repairs are more expensive than ever, then this is a large part of the answer.

Now of course our public services are just that: services. Hospitals, schools, and old-peoples' homes are precisely the kinds of places whose productivity it is hard to raise above their trend rates. Technology can make some difference, it is true; lectures can be webcast, x-rays can be emailed, day surgery can replace long periods in hospital. But the scope to increase productivity in services is much less than in manufacturing. Moreover, it is not always clear why you would even want to automate services, as anyone who has ever called an automated telephone system will testify. Proper care and attention is what many of these services are about; it's what makes them valuable. Nurses cannot tend to patients, nor can teachers mark essays, much faster now than twenty years ago; or if they can, perhaps they should not.

Baumol's cost disease is no-one's fault; it is just an economic fact of life. But it raises the stakes of the present discussion in three ways. First, it makes clear why the problems identified here must be an inescapable and long-term part of the wider political debate. Secondly, it underlines the costs of recent public policy: the cost of the state's inability to keep public sector productivity near the UK's long-term trend growth rate; and the degree to which its recent policy of state growth without state reform has missed the opportunity to make structural changes while there was still money and time to do so. Finally, even once current inefficiencies in state delivery are addressed, Baumol's cost disease will put huge long-term upward pressure on tax revenues as a percentage of GDP. It makes it impossible to dodge the question of whether the state should continue to provide the services it does over the longer term.

Beyond the State

For these reasons, then, our present reliance on the state will prove unsustainable over time. In the words of WB Yeats, the centre cannot hold. We are over-wedded as a nation to the state, and to a single centralised model of public service provision, and the effect is to impose a huge and growing burden of risk on all of us.

We need to think beyond the state. This claim may once have seemed quaint, irrelevant or alarmist. In the current fiscal crisis, it has become more widely shared. But this crisis, like the massive boom that preceded it, will pass in due course. The real question is whether we will have learned the lessons of our overreliance; and whether the new emerging order has the energy, the creativity and the ideas needed to sustain this country in future decades.

This is the economic context for the Big Society. In the next chapter we turn to its social context. Here too economics, and specifically the conventional economics of the old textbooks, casts a long shadow. But the focus will be not on the limitations of the state, but on how we, and our government, misunderstand human nature itself.

3 A Fracture in Society

She looked over his shoulder
For vines and olive trees,
Marble well-governed cities
And ships upon untamed seas,
But there on the shining metal
His hands had put instead
An artificial wilderness
And a sky like lead.

A plain without a feature, bare and brown,
No blade of grass, no sign of neighbourhood,
Nothing to eat and nowhere to sit down,
Yet, congregated on its blankness, stood
An unintelligible multitude,
A million eyes, a million boots in line,
Without expression, waiting for a sign.

WH Auden, The Shield of Achilles

Auden begins at the moment in the *Iliad* when Homer describes the shield that Hephaestus has wrought for Achilles, before Achilles' climactic battle with the Trojan prince Hector. On the shield are set forth the heavens, the ocean, scenes of farming and dancing, and two great cities. One city is at peace, with a wedding and a legal dispute in progress. The other is at war, under siege and with a battle raging. It is a supreme metaphor for society as a whole: for humanity and nature, for order and disorder, for reason and emotion, for law and the chaos of combat.

Yet in one respect at least, Auden betters it. For in his poem the opposite of order is not disorder, but emptiness: the fields denuded of crops, no life or love or wit or human purpose, individuals swallowed up in an aimless crowd. Society has lost its meaning. Homer has life and death, yet Auden's image of nothingness and utter vulnerability is the more chilling.

Current concerns about British society are far removed from Auden. Yet even before the idea of a Big Society started to gain currency a deep worry had become evident: a kind of moral panic about where our society is headed and what it is becoming. It could be seen in concern about social indicators such as drug abuse and teenage pregnancy. It could be seen in a widespread fear that towns and cities are losing their local character and the whole country its distinctive national identity. It could be seen in a lack of trust, and in feelings that those in power are distant, unaccountable for their actions and unable to change what needs to be changed. And it could be seen in a growing belief that basic values are being lost in consumerism and a money culture.

These worries do not lack evidence. For example, the UK underperforms other EU countries across a wide range of social indicators: we have had the highest drug use in Europe for a decade in almost every major category, including cocaine, amphetamines, ecstasy and cannabis. We have by far the highest levels of binge drinking of the larger European countries. We have the worst record for teenage pregnancy, and the highest proportion of children in houses without work.

The position of young people is an especially telling indicator of what the future has in store. A 2007 report by UNICEF showed Britain near the bottom of 21 countries in the material and educational wellbeing of children; and lowest of all in self-esteem, unhealthy behaviour and quality of family and peer relationships. A further study found that more than 1.2 million 16-to 24-year-olds in England, Scotland and Wales, or just under one in five, are not in employment, education or training (NEET). In the 16- to 19-year-old bracket, the figure is 11%—twice that in Germany and France. Most recently, it was reported that one in ten children under the age of five is obese.

To make matters worse, these social problems do not fall evenly on the population. In general, the poor fare worse than the rich, the sick worse than the healthy, the old (and very young) worse than the young, those from ethnic minorities worse than whites. Social decline is thus highly socially regressive, compounding the effect of growing wealth and income inequalities. But all have been affected to some degree: a major poll by *The Observer* in May 2007 revealed that on balance respondents believed that Britain then was less successful, less pleasant, more dangerous, less liberal and a lot less happy than in 1997.

The different impact of social factors is especially marked between old and young. Those born in the 1950s—the generation of Tony Blair and Gordon Brown—found a Britain of relative social cohesion and security. They grew up when the NHS was still basking in its postwar glory, offering the best healthcare in the world equally to all, and free of charge. Relatively few enjoyed a university education but those that did paid nothing, indeed they were subsidised to attend. Jobs came with secure employment and rewarding pensions based on final salaries. An average couple could expect to buy their first house in their twenties. Foreign conflicts stayed foreign. Until the emergence of the provisional IRA there was little threat of bombs on British streets. Crime was low.

These advantages did not and could not last. While it would be absurd to be dewy-eyed with nostalgia for the 1950s, those growing up today enjoy few of them now. They will pay—a lot—towards their own higher education, and leave with significant debt. They will be treated by an NHS that has been overtaken in quality and results by its international peers. They will enter a jobs market which is ever more internationally competitive. They will have to change jobs and retrain several times in the course of a lifetime. They will likely buy a flat, not a house, and that in their thirties. They will grow up in a country where drug abuse is common, and where there is widespread fear of terrorism and violent crime. No wonder an excellent recent analysis of the situation of young people was called *Jilted Generation*.

In response to these problems, the British government has not distinguished itself either by policy or action. On the contrary, in social as well as in economic policy, the negative effects of recent state growth and centralisation are evident. They often stand in the way of better public services, and they embody an often profoundly insulting attitude to the ordinary citizen.

The true picture has been greatly obscured by political rhetoric. In particular, under Tony Blair Labour managed to accrue tremendous political capital by defining itself as the party of compassion and "social justice" against the supposedly uncaring Conservatives. It made undeniable and important strides in the treatment of minorities and discrimination. Viewed in the round, however, its own record on social justice—however we define it—was itself greatly flawed.

Take inequality, for example. On the standard economic measure, the heavy redistribution of income between 1997 and 2008 made almost no improvement to overall economic equality. Indeed it got slightly worse over the period. But this in itself is cause for concern. If a serious and thoroughgoing attempt to redistribute income cannot make real overall gains during the longest period of British peacetime prosperity in recorded history, this in itself highlights the severity of the long-term challenge and the need for new thinking.

Meanwhile, despite some positive achievements, we should also note that in many ways the expansion of the state under Labour actively undermined social justice. It resulted in an incredibly complex benefits system that the poor struggle to understand; a savings system that often deterred saving; police forces that increasingly faced inwards, not outwards to deprived local communities; "baby bonds" that, originally at least, paid twelve times as much money to well-off children as to poor ones; a housing system that was slanted towards smaller flats and less green space; schools that had more new buildings but less freedom to teach; a criminal justice system that offered less access to the victims of crime; and an NHS that struggled to raise its performance in the knowledge that weakening productivity in fact meant fewer operations, less treatment, more sickness and earlier death.

Britain has been estimated to have 4.2 million security cameras, more than any country in the world except Communist China. Some of the most basic rights of British citizens have been deliberately eroded, while a host of new regulations encourage petty dishonesty and fraud. Social mobility has declined. Meanwhile, 3.8 million more people in Great Britain have been brought into the tax system, 2.7

million of them among the less well-off, and the poorest quintile of the population pays a higher percentage of its income in tax than the richest. Where is the social justice in all this?

It is perhaps not surprising, then, that popular trust in government itself has been at a record low, even before the recent scandal over parliamentary expenses. This is not just a matter of falling turnout in elections. What is of special concern is how this disengagement splits broadly along the lines of age, ethnicity and income. In the 2005 General Election, only 37% of 18-24 year-olds voted, as opposed to 75% of those over 65. Among those of black or ethnic minority background, 47% voted; among whites, 62% did. Among those categorised in social classes D and E, 54% voted; among those in classes A and B, 70% did.

Contrary to much received wisdom, for these groups the point is not the supposed difficulty of voting. Nor is it simply that voters do not care about the issues of the day; they do, as we can see from single-issue politics, which is flourishing. No, the question for many people is whether it is worth voting at all. It seems as though the basic social contract—the implicit deal by which people trade social engagement for security—is starting to fall apart. Instead of elected representatives, they see a homogeneous political and media class which has lost its democratic connection with ordinary voters; and so lost the political legitimacy and authenticity which democracy creates.

The Unholy Alliance

Why has this happened? Those on the left of the political spectrum have attributed this social decomposition to what they see as the selfish individualism and inequality created by Thatcherism. Those on the right have cited, among other things, poor long-term economic management, the growth of permissive legislation, and the decline of the Church.

Yet at a deeper level there is another and more subtle phenomenon also at work. This lies in the embedded assumptions about economics, indeed about human nature itself, to be found in British public administration. This understanding is revealed in policy, in government behaviour and in a series of explicit background papers on economic analysis such as the Treasury's *Green Book: Appraisal and Evaluation in Central Government*. What they show, broadly speaking, is that British government is in the grip of a highly damaging and outdated 1970s textbook conception of economics.

It is this textbook approach that has underpinned and legitimised many of the policies and much of the centralisation and state growth already noted. It has had the effect of making the recent obsession with top-down tinkering and micro-management seem not merely appropriate, but positively required. And at the same time, as we shall see, it has encouraged a politically useful belief in unfettered financial markets, so that wise, active and hands-on regulation of banks by practitioners has been replaced by a culture of box-checking.

This standard economics treats human beings as purely self-interested, endlessly calculating costs and benefits, and highly sensitive to marginal gains and losses. It is extremely mathematical, and canonically expressed not in language but in the equations of calculus and statistics. We will explore this way of thinking below, and analyse its strengths and weaknesses in detail. But the key point is that it exercises an undetected monopoly of policy ideas and policy tools in the minds of many of our top civil servants and politicians. And like all monopolies, this one has malign consequences.

Tax Credits

The present tax credit system is a perfect example of this bad thinking in action. The idea of a negative income tax was advanced as early as the 1960s by Geoffrey Howe, based on an original suggestion of Milton Friedman. It has been regularly considered by different chancellors since then and rejected, mainly on the grounds of complexity, before being launched in the form of tax credits by Gordon Brown as Chancellor in 2003.

Tax credits are means-tested payments, and so are geared to the recipients' income. As that income changes, it is inevitable that in some cases under- or overpayments will occur. But it makes a huge difference if the system chosen tops up income before or after the income is actually received. If it is topped up afterwards, then a family may have too low an income for a period before the top-up. But if the tax credit gets paid in advance, then the system becomes far more complex and overpayments—and, since this is public money, the need for government to reclaim them later—become far more likely. How to design such a system is, then, a political and administrative judgement call.

Various different overall approaches have been tried over the years in the US, Canada and Australia. So a large amount of previous experience and knowledge about tax credit systems was available. But as Chancellor Mr Brown did not adopt any of these approaches. Instead he decided to innovate, and to create a new, predictive and so highly complex tax credits payments system of his own, managed not from the Department of Work and Pensions but from the small and administratively inexperienced Treasury itself.

The results have been disastrous. The House of Commons Public Accounts Committee found in 2008 that the Government had overpaid £6 billion in the first three years of the system operation. A total of £2.3 billion had been wasted—enough, for example, to maintain the current public subsidy to the Post Office network for some 15 years.

During this period overpayments affected 1.9 million families (roughly one-third of those involved), not the originally projected 750,000. Some of these families were then thrust into debt as the state attempted to recover the public money already paid out. And what was almost worse: the system was so open, indeed encouraging, to fraud and abuse that it was discovered that 200,000 more single parents claimed tax credits than the Office of National Statistics believe are in existence.

It might seem absurd to say that part of the problem with tax credits was that their creators had a poor understanding of economics. Yet it is true, and that reliance had three disastrous effects. The first was that they wrongly assumed that ordinary people would actually understand and be able to react rationally to massive complexities of the new system—in other words, they assumed people were far more economically rational than they actually are. In fact, the system is so complex that even experts have had great difficulty in understanding it.

The second effect was to focus attention at the margin: not on the mass of people who would be helped in their lives by a simple policy, but on the small number of extra ones who would be helped, or helped more, by a more complex one. For the argument was made: while we are looking after the core, why not look after them too? After all, they had needs—often very serious ones—and the additional complexity involved did not register in the model and so had no quantifiable cost. And of course these extra people were also voters. But if these were helped, then why not target the next group, and the next…?

This is how a focus on marginal cases naturally tends to increase complexity, and woo the policymaker into error. Of course a balance needs to be struck. But complexity naturally breeds waste, and creates new temptation for people to defraud the system. Thus can an economic decision have unexpected social and moral side-effects.

The final effect of the standard approach was to create more disruption when, as many predicted, the system went wrong. In orthodox economics, people are assumed to have equal and opposite reactions to gain or loss. But research from the 1990s in behavioural economics suggests that actually this is not true. In fact people are generally loss-averse: that is, they have a greater desire (roughly twice as great) to avoid loss than to make profit. The tax credits system did not recognise this. It created unexpected losses for a huge number of people, when Government sought to reclaim previous overpayments from them. It thus made a significant, continuing and largely avoidable contribution to human suffering.

The Discontents of Capitalism

Yet this is only half the picture. Failed policy and fears of social decline are not the only causes of loss of trust. Public concern runs far wider than this, to include feelings of loss of place, of value, of accountability and control. Walk through almost any city or town today and you see the effects of "clone town Britain", where high streets have been replaced by malls or superstores, and individual shops by a monochrome strip of global and national chains: one might be anywhere. Local values, customs and traditions have been superseded by national sales programmes. And little local power exists to question or influence these changes, especially once they have occurred.

Many of these fears are reflected by and through the green movement, and focuses on the effects of a go-faster, have-it-all society: on stress, poor health, noise, traffic congestion, sprawl and pollution. This new awareness has massively raised people's grasp of their own costs to others and to the planet.

But even among those who care nothing for the environment, there is the sense that something is wrong: that in some way human identity and human character are being lost in the face of a Gresham's law in which a money culture displaces other priorities and traditional values. And many people have been tempted to think that the deepest problem lies not in individual or even national actions, but in the system of global corporate capitalism itself. It is supposedly this system that exalts values of greed and acquisitiveness in people. It is this system that has liberated economic forces which now sweep across the globe. And against this system even nations are, it is believed, powerless.

This line of thought mistakenly assumes that there is only one variety of capitalism, as we shall see. But whether or not you agree with it, the motivating concern that human character is increasingly driven by greed and fear is important. We have already noted that British government suffers from a faulty understanding of economics. But this is also true of our fundamental grasp of human behaviour. As a society we increasingly seem to believe that human beings are basically economic, rather than social, animals: that their behaviour is always motivated, and so to be explained, by self-interest and the desire for gain. On this view, people are calculating machines, always assessing the odds and the possibilities for gain. They always want more wealth, power and status. And so they fix their attention on the margin, where net cost yields to net benefit.

This view of human beings is very seductive, and in recent decades it has received huge cultural reinforcement from a wide range of sources. The media have endlessly promoted it, as though football transfers and Big Brother were the only form of human interaction. But most of all it has fed off itself. For once people start to see each other as merely economically or financially motivated, they treat them so. And once they are so treated, they themselves will tend to behave in the same pounds-shillings-and-pence way. And so it goes on.

But two other factors have also played a role. The first is the simple point that any action can in principle be "explained" through self-interest. Why do people act altruistically? Not because they want to help others, but because it makes them feel good. Why are soldiers prepared to die in battle? Not because they love their mates or believe in a cause, but for personal prestige or family glory. Why did that politician do that? Not because of her character or ideals or sense of vocation, but because she's on the take. All very convenient—although a theory that purports to explain everything in fact explains nothing.

But confusingly, the self-interest view can also of course offer genuine and useful explanations. Everyone behaves selfishly sometimes, and some people do so often. Even more confusingly, the self-interest view can sometimes explain, and occasionally predict, aggregate human behaviour very well. That's what so much of modern economics is about.

Nevertheless, as a default view of human motivation, the self-interest view is profoundly and dangerously inadequate, as we shall see. But first we need to get clear on how it arose in the first place. How did we get here? How did this economic idea of humanity achieve its present cultural pre-eminence and status in the public mind?

Enter Homo Economicus

The idea that people are purely economically self-interested has some of its earliest roots in the thought of the Greek philosopher Epicurus. But its present status is the creation of the last three centuries. It arose from the professionalisation of economics as an academic discipline.

It is only slightly unfair to say that economics as a discipline started with Adam Smith and *The Wealth of Nations* in 1776. But economics was not invented by Smith. Rather, he created a systematic account from many already-current economic arguments and ideas. For example, many people would probably associate the words "laissez-faire" with Smithian economics. But in fact they were coined by Mirabeau and it was the French physiocrats, first and foremost François Quesnay, who developed many of the key economic ideas of the time. Smith's genius lay in bringing these ideas together and uniting them in a new body of thought.

Smith may have been the first modern economist, but he did not regard himself as one. Rather he saw himself as a moral philosopher, as a legal scholar and (in effect) as a social scientist. Thus he dealt with economic problems and ideas, but only in their wider social, historical and political contexts. And he certainly did not believe that human beings were purely selfish. Indeed he wrote *The Theory of Moral Sentiments* in 1759 to argue for the quite different and opposed view that sympathy or compassion was the psychological basis of personal morality.

The Theory of Moral Sentiments opens with the following lines:

> *How selfish soever man may be supposed, there are evidently some principles in his nature, which interest him in the fortunes of others, and render their happiness necessary to him,*

> *though he derives nothing from it, except the pleasure of seeing*
> *it. Of this kind is pity or compassion, the emotion we feel for*
> *the misery of others, when we either see it, or are made to con-*
> *ceive it in a very lively manner.*

In the Smithian view, personal morality and social norms arise from a process of imagining and reconstructing the experience of others. What matters is not compassion as pity, but compassion as fellow-feeling. Of this view the present book is a distant, modest but direct descendent.

To return. For more than a hundred years after Smith, the greatest economic thinkers came from a wide variety of backgrounds: David Ricardo was a stockbroker, Leon Walras a mathematician, William Stanley Jevons a natural scientist, and Carl Menger a lawyer. The last economist who had a comparable universal education was Friedrich Hayek, who trained as both a lawyer and an economist but also published in the areas of psychology and political philosophy. And it was Hayek who once remarked that nobody can be a great economist who is only an economist.

Both intellectually and in practice, then, the earliest economic thinking was embedded in society, and nowhere is this clearer than in the works of Adam Smith himself. But one need only look at any of today's standard economics textbooks to see that something has drastically changed since then. In fact many modern economics textbooks look rather like introductions to physics or mathematics. They are full of formulae and graphs, they use words like "equilibria" and "elasticity", but they often shun any reference to historical, social or political facts. So what has changed? And why?

In *The Wealth of Nations* Smith had presented us with a verbal description of the workings of the market economy. It was published at a crucial point in British history, in which the scientific advances of the Enlightenment were being used to drive the Industrial Revolution. Economists looked with amazement at the new steam engines, at railways, at electricity. And they noted that economics had not built any steam engines or railways; indeed it could not point at that time to any major achievement at all.

The early economists thus naturally looked up to the exact sciences. In particular they looked up to Newton's towering work, *Principia Mathematica*, which seemed the definitive statement of the laws of physics, and which expressed those laws in mathematical form in the manner of Euclid's geometry. So what could be more natural than a desire to mimic the natural sciences, with their elegant mathematical methods, their rigorous measurements and their astonishing capacity for prediction? And this meant one thing above all: the full-scale deployment of the latest mathematical techniques.

Take markets, for example. In Adam Smith's work there are many analyses of markets and the different ways in which they work. Yet during the 19th Century such verbal accounts were increasingly thought to be insufficiently precise. Starting with the French mathematician Cournot, a concerted attempt was made to improve on this assumed inadequacy of Smith. The result of the work of generations of economists since then has been to introduce various mathematically specified characteristics which have to be present to make a market work in theory: for example, to bring supply and demand into an efficient equilibrium.

This mathematical tendency arose from and reinforced a desire to move economics away from the messy detail of commercial society, which was all but impossible to model in equations, and into the more congenial atmosphere of theoretical abstraction. And it was blessed by

John Stuart Mill, who was the very model of the 19th Century liberal public intellectual. Political economy, said Mill "does not treat of the whole of man's nature as modified by the social state, nor of the whole conduct of man in society. It is concerned with him solely as a being who desires to possess wealth, and who is capable of judging of the comparative efficacy of means for obtaining that end. It predicts only such of the phenomena of the social state as take place in consequence of the pursuit of wealth. It makes entire abstraction of every other human passion or motive." Thus was society publicly abolished from economic thought—and by the leading liberal thinker of the period, no less.

This process of making economics more mathematical took a major step forward with the publication of Alfred Marshall's great synthesis, *The Principles of Economics*, in 1890. Yet although Marshall himself strongly believed in the importance of mathematical rigour, he also knew that graphs and equations would deter the average reader. For him mathematics was a short-cut, a heuristic used to reach results whose final expression must be in plain English using real examples.

In part as a result, Marshall's book was a huge success, whose influence stretched to the Second World War. And that success was repeated after the war by Paul Samuelson with his famous textbook *Economics* in 1948. *Economics* was a comprehensive presentation of broadly neoclassical economics from first principles. In many ways it updated, refined and extended the work of Marshall. Yet it also differed in two crucial ways. The first was in content. The interwar period had seen the triumph of John Maynard Keynes and his ideas of activist government. In his General Theory, and in his own role as government adviser, Keynes had given a master-class in showing how an economic theory, vigorously advocated, could have profound effects on policy.

According to the not naturally modest Keynes and his acolytes, his theory finally achieved what economists had long dreamt of. It explained the cause of the British interwar economic malaise, as too little demand in the face of huge unemployment, resulting in stagnation. But it also gave a prescription to government as to how to cure the problem, through large-scale state spending and conscious targeting of full employment. This has given Keynes heroic status on the political left, though in many respects—notably his emphasis on the inevitable uncertainty of human life, his pragmatism and his attention to how people actually behave— Keynes was actually rather conservative in spirit.

Samuelson's book was also a presentational tour de force, showing how Keynes's ideas could be incorporated within a neoclassical framework. Thus was born a policy consensus that lasted until the 1970s, and a theoretical picture of economics that remains broadly in place in the public mind today.

One further event deserves brief mention in this potted history. That is the publication of *The Calculus of Consent* by James Buchanan and Gordon Tullock in 1962. This book effectively launched what has become known as Public Choice theory, or the application of economic principles to political matters such as voting, the working of special interest groups and the behaviour of politicians. Its special significance for this discussion lies in two things. First, in the fact that it took much political explanation to be founded on the basis of economics; and second, in its assumption that politicians and bureaucrats, far from following any vocation or devotion to public service as they often professed, were in fact purely economically motivated. The effect of this was to repudiate the emphasis on civic virtue and on the political life as a calling that had existed within republican political theory ever since Aristotle. Thus was politics logically subordinated to economics, and the theoretical justification laid for centuries of voter disgust, before and afterwards, with politicians and public servants.

For his part, Paul Samuelson shared Marshall's passion for rigour. But unlike Marshall he saw himself as writing less for the common man and more for a (semi-) professional audience of undergraduates and academics. He was thus quite willing to use ideas, metaphors and techniques from mathematics and physics, which contributed to the sense that here was something privileged, expert and important. The overall result, reinforced by Samuelson's Nobel Prize in 1970, was a huge leap in the intellectual prestige and popular fame of economics as a subject. Universities widely adopted Samuelson's book, in the UK as in the USA; undergraduates scratched their heads and occasionally absorbed it; and some of those undergraduates became today's politicians, civil servants and policy wonks.

There is one other and more melancholy point of continuity. In their desire to present a comprehensive and unified synthesis of their subject, both Marshall and Samuelson downplayed the existence of dissident voices and competing points of view. The effect was to reinforce the sense of an orthodoxy within economics, and this in turn heavily shaped the research agenda and fed into tenure decisions within the universities.

The Return to Reality

Yet in fact 1970 can also be seen as the high water mark, the point at which academic economic orthodoxy started to change, fragment and reassemble itself. It was almost exactly at this time that economics as a profession started to turn back to reality. True, the subject became ever more relentlessly mathematical. But the target changed: since then the use for economic theory to describe and predict actual human behaviour better has become a central preoccupation of the discipline. Well-known examples of this include Daniel Kahneman and Amos Tversky's use of cognitive psychology to explain common mistakes in human rationality, Gary Becker's extension of economics into sociology, crime and family dynamics, and George Akerlof's examination of the effect of asymmetric information on markets. But there are many others.

The present public understanding of economics, however, reflects few if any of these changes. On the contrary, it remains rooted in the textbooks of the 1970s. The present situation thus piles irony upon irony. The more mathematical economics became, the less well-understood it was by the average person whose behaviour it sought to explain. The less well-understood it was, the greater grew its prestige. The greater its prestige, the more people wanted to study it. A theory dedicated to explaining markets and competition achieved a virtual monopoly in its own marketplace. With every shift along this path, economic theory moved further away from the real world. And just at its apogee, at its point of greatest distance from human life in all its infinite variety, that standard economics entered British government and the British public consciousness. And there it has remained, and grown.

In this worldview, as Mill wished, every contextual element has been purged from Adam Smith's original account. Time, place and people no longer exist. Reason is reduced to mere calculation. What remains is a perfect world, with perfect markets shaped by perfect competition: an economic version of Nirvana that has little if anything to do with the world we see around us every day.

Instead there is, in Auden's words, not olives, vines and well-governed cities, but *An artificial wilderness / And a sky like lead. / A plain without a feature, bare and brown, / No blade of grass, no sign of neighbourhood. / Nothing to eat and nowhere to sit down.* It is a towering technical achievement. But if our understanding of economics relies purely on it, then that understanding is grossly and dangerously deficient.

The Big Society contains within it a far more positive and persuasive alternative view, both of human nature and of the sources of human wealth and well-being. But first we need to look at the basic assumptions of this economic view of mankind more closely.

4 *Rigor Mortis* Economics

Mathematics brought rigor to Economics.
Unfortunately, it also brought mortis.
Kenneth E. Boulding

It's late afternoon. You're in the office and need to work. But the sun is shining and your friends are having a picnic. You know the beer is warming up with every passing minute. What to do?

Luckily, you have in the back of your mind a rather rusty PhD in neoclassical economics. That theory says that you will work up until the point when your benefit from more work is exactly counterbalanced by your loss at not going out with your mates. After sketching a few graphs, setting up a spreadsheet and using your trusty skills in calculus, you decide the tipping point is 5.47 pm. At that time, off you go.

OK, so the last bit is a caricature. But it reminds us that this kind of general thinking, trading off costs and benefits up to a marginal point where they are equal, is absolutely commonplace. We do it every day, in hundreds of different ways. And we typically do not think of it as economic thinking at all. It's just about planning and running our lives.

Conventional economics is in part a highly technical theory about how people make these decisions. It has many merits. But one of its unintended effects has been to stifle our society, by distorting public policy and encouraging us to view ourselves and each other as economic automata. We can think of it as making three key assumptions. The first is that people have perfectly rational preferences among different outcomes; this means, for example, that if they prefer A to B and B to C, then they prefer A to C. The second is that individuals maximise their utility, or gain, or benefit; and firms maximise their profits. And the third is that they act independently of each other, on the basis of perfect information. All of these have echoes in the example above.

The core assumptions, like those in the natural sciences, are idealised generalisations. They do not purport to describe what people are actually like, only to be useful simplifications. The idea is that people's differences balance themselves out in the aggregate, so that the theory looks to generate rich explanations and predictive power by treating people as if they were perfectly rational utility-maximisers operating under perfect information.

Now you often hear people say about this picture, with a knowing smile: "Ah yes, but it's completely flawed, because no-one is really like that". But this criticism misses its target. Our standard economics is not a theory about how individual people actually are, only about how they behave overall. By analogy: for centuries after Newton, physics made the assumption that gravitational force was always exercised from a point at the centre of a given body. It may not have been true, but it made for some stunning predictions. The really damaging criticism is not that "no-one is really like that". It is that even in the aggregate people systematically do not behave as the standard model predicts.

Of course, people do not live in a vacuum; they constantly deal and trade with each other, through markets. And these markets use prices to show the relative scarcity of the goods and services traded.

Prices are signals from people and households to firms to show what they want, and from firms to households and people to show how much those things cost. When supply and demand balance out, then a market is conventionally said to be in equilibrium.

But the greatest claim of the theory lies at the level not of the individual or the market, but at that of an economy as a whole. For economists have been able to show in a formal, mathematical way under certain very specific conditions that a market economy which is in competitive equilibrium is maximally efficient. Moreover, such an economy maximises the utility or benefit of the people in it. No-one can be made better off without someone else being made worse off. Adam Smith's invisible hand thus creates not merely the greatest aggregate efficiency, but the greatest overall utility as well. That's quite a result.

This approach has been filled out over time with detail, and with specific tools. Two of these deserve mention: discounted cash flow analysis and cost-benefit analysis. Discounted cash flow analysis is a mathematical tool by which to estimate the value today of cash payments in the future, or vice versa. It reflects a standard assumption that capital sums and income streams can be treated equivalently. Cost-benefit analysis is a formal technique of project appraisal, which values the expenses and expected returns of a project in monetary terms to establish a net positive or negative contribution. Both approaches are very widely used within government and in the private sector. Within government they have been heavily promoted and exhaustively analysed, especially within the Treasury and within successive departments of the environment and health.

This, then, is the traditional picture. It has become our conventional economic worldview. In the economics profession it is often called the Standard Economic Model or SEM. If we needed an –ism we might call it economism, but *rigor mortis* economics is perhaps still better. As a formal theory it is a work of great beauty and genius. But it has many weaknesses. Much of its actual real-world value is illusory. Some of its consequences are positively dangerous. And its hold on the public mind is bunk. Economic theories are not religious monoliths but tools of description, explanation and prediction. This textbook economics is not the only game in town. There are other theories, and other ways we should be thinking about people and their behaviour, yet to be considered.

Take the recent global financial crash. At its deepest level, the crash arose because people and markets did not behave in the standard way described in the economic textbooks. First, people are not always economically rational: in this case, they massively overborrowed to buy houses, and then remortgaged those houses to buy other things. Second, free markets are not always efficient: in this case, they mispriced credit as banks hyped 125% mortgages and other debt products to a credulous public, then mispriced it again as the wholesale markets were unable to work out how much different mortgage assets were worth, leading to the wholesale equivalent of a run on the banks. And finally, poorly conceived policy and poorly crafted institutions can fail: in this case, there has been a huge institutional failure within the regulatory system, and in government oversight of the economy. Thus at every level, the crash arose because people, markets and institutions did not behave as the old textbooks would have us believe.

And one point in particular is worth noting. The present picture implies that any derogation from perfect competition in a market economy creates inefficiency and makes some people worse off. So socialism must fail. But so too must rational debate about different varieties of capitalism. For on this account there can only be one, hyper-libertarian, variety of capitalism. In other words, just at the point when we need an intelligent debate about how the UK and other modern market economies should develop, our most basic economic theory seems to make that debate impossible.

Unpicking the Assumptions

In fact, however, the standard economic model is nothing like as robust as it appears. At its core is a set of ideas each of which has been severely questioned by professional economists over the past 30 years. But what is so striking is the intellectual hold which the standard model continues to exert on public policy and on British society as a whole. In this chapter, then, we look more closely at the weaknesses of the standard model, and at its damaging effects—including its role in the recent financial crisis.

Perfect Competition?

We start with the analysis of markets. According to textbook economic theory, markets produce efficient results, but only if they fulfil certain formal criteria. There must be myriads of buyers and sellers, whose identity is unknown, each of whom is omniscient about market information and each too small to have an influence on the market price. What is traded on the market must be homogeneous, that is, exactly identical: there can be no branding or even provenance such as "Jaffa orange juice", for example. These theoretical markets supposedly react instantly to any change in supply and demand, so that there are no processes that take place over time. In an economy, there is deemed to be a complete set of perfectly competitive markets, for all goods, everywhere and always.

In other words, these markets occupy no time and no place. Moreover, for the same reason, there are no human accretions in this picture: no institutions, no practices, no rules or traditions, no moral or ethical standards, no emotions, no human relations, no altruism or fellow-feeling, no philanthropy, no rule of law, no history, no culture.

However, many economics textbooks tend to use the model of perfect competition as a prescription for what markets ought to be. Take the latest edition of Samuelson's *Economics*, one of the best-selling economics text-books ever written. After listing the requirements of perfectly competitive markets and claiming that only such markets can lead to efficient outcomes, the authors write: "Alas, there are many ways that markets can fall short of perfect competition ... Market failure leads to inefficient production or consumption, and government can play a role in curing the disease." In other words, reality is seen through the spectacles of formal economic models. Discrepancies between reality and the idealised models are then seen as some sort of imperfection—but an imperfection in reality, not in the model.

In the real world, of course, the key assumptions of textbook economics are rarely even closely approximated. But the effect of this formalisation is to exclude from the theory roughly all of the things that give human life its point and meaning. A world without culture is a world without music and joy. A world without moral standards is a world without personal obligation, honour or duty. A world without institutions is a world without families, clubs and reunions. A world without emotion is a world without love or friendship or trust.

It is also a million miles away from Adam Smith. For Adam Smith, capitalism is not a form of desiccated economic atomism. He recognises the workings of the invisible hand, of course, but he also recognises the human capacity for sympathy or compassion. So Smith sees markets not as disembodied but as operating within a rich local cultural context which embraces individual moral beliefs, a person's own energy, flair and imagination, unstated background assumptions as to honesty and fair dealing, and a shared understanding of market conventions, institutions and traditions. In short, the Edinburgh of the 1770s.

Perfect Information?

We can go further. Part of the beauty of market economies today is precisely that they do *not* obey the assumptions of the standard model; and yet in many ways they still function remarkably well. Thus consumers do not need perfect information about goods traded in the market. On the contrary, they may know virtually nothing about them. But they can still generally rely on markets and the division of labour to meet their demand at a given price. Mrs Bloggs may not have tea plants or the steady sunshine of Darjeeling at her disposal. She may think tea is an oil by-product made by human slaves on the planet Venus. But if she has the right cash she can buy a pack of PG Tips whenever she chooses.

Not only that: there is reason to think markets actually require imperfect information in order to work properly. For if markets always contained perfect information, no-one would or could have an incentive to find out more. Similarly, if all technological insights were immediately available to others, no inventor would have an economic incentive to innovate, and innovation would cease. The effect of assuming perfect competition and market equilibrium is thus in fact to prevent any competition from taking place at all.

This is a major weakness in the conventional theory, because it strikes at the heart of a basic assumption about information. But its value does not cease there. For it also draws attention to the static, arrested nature of the theory as a whole. It suggests that there are no such things as equilibria in economics, as in nature; that everything is on the hop and in flux; and that markets in particular are dynamic, liquid movements that cannot be properly understood in static terms. In the real world, of course, this is not news.

Rationality, Behavioural Economics and the Financial Crash

These assumptions about markets and information are fundamental to the standard economic model. It would be silly to think that they would, could or should ever go unanswered. On the contrary, there has long been a flourishing trade within the academic world of economics in examining what happens when they are changed and deliberately imperfect assumptions are made instead.

The same is true for the standard assumption that individuals are perfectly economically rational, and the most important line of criticism for the present discussion targets this assumption. That criticism is largely based on behavioural economics, which draws on insights from human psychology. We saw earlier how standard economics wrongly assumes that people are equally geared to gain and loss, whereas in fact they have a disproportionate aversion to loss. Recent research has shown many other flaws in the assumption of perfect rationality. People systematically behave quite differently, and more interestingly, than the standard expectation would suggest.

We do not need to enter the laboratory to see evidence that humans are not fully economically rational. Consider the financial markets, which are often taken to be the paradigm of market activity. Even well-informed financial investors often behave irrationally. They get caught up in fads, they follow financial snake-oil salesmen, they obsessively chart price movements, they fail to diversify their portfolios and they churn their shares, for example. Markets can be inefficient, they can misprice risk and reward, and they can overshoot for reasons of fashion or sentiment on the way up or down.

But this is merely anecdotal. What is more interesting is research which shows that people are not randomly economically irrational, but follow fairly consistent patterns. Thus there is strong evidence that people are biased towards the present and status quo, even in the face of positive reason to change their view; that they cue their reactions off key reference points, rather than by systematically evaluating the alternatives; that they place a higher value on objects they own than on new ones; and that rather than seeing money as always and everywhere the same, or capital as simply equivalent to deferred income, they run their finances by thinking in terms of different pots of money or "mental accounts".

Not only that: how people take decisions is heavily influenced by the way those decisions are framed, so that they choose one option when a given choice is framed positively and another when negatively. They also think of risk and reward in terms of available and salient examples, so that the probability of someone's dying in a tornado is rated higher than, say, from asthma (in fact in the US at least the latter is twenty times more probable). All of these types of behaviour violate the rules of rationality assumed by textbook economics. But few will come as a deep surprise to those who reflect on their own behaviour, or who have studied modern marketing techniques. For many of those techniques are designed to exploit precisely these features of human psychology.

There is now a huge literature on behavioural economics, much of which is directly relevant to public policy. The fact that people tend to think of money in different mental accounts, for example, is of great significance for future reform of the benefit system. But the key point is simply this: in the absence of definite information human beings often make very poor judgements about what to do.

The recent financial crisis makes the case perfectly. It seems likely that the housing boom was fuelled by a range of features of human psychology which encouraged buyers to make poor choices. On this view, individuals' natural bias towards the present inclined them to accept teaser mortgages from banks offering very low rates for an initial period but at a much higher later cost. As values started to rise, other buyers were cued or competitively encouraged to enter the market who would not have done so otherwise, even at the higher prices. They were further stimulated because of the known tendency of people to overestimate their ability to save for the future, and their reluctance to realise a loss. Once the boom was established, house owners' appetite for risk may also have risen because they were already sitting on large unrealised capital gains, fuelling further price rises.

Moreover, it may well be that the continuance of low interest rates created a perception that the world had in fact become less risky than it was. And above all there was also a competitive me-too instinct not to miss out on the boom, but keep up with others. As the groundswell of demand grew, any anchor which prices might have had in fundamental values dropped away, and it became in no-one's interest to question or attempt to correct further rises. The result was galloping and unsustainable house price inflation, and a disproportionately greater final crash.

Bad Influence, Bad Policy

Let us review the discussion so far. Both an argument from first principles and recent empirical research suggest that the standard model is intellectually unsustainable. There is good reason to implicate it as a prime cause of the recent housing boom and bust. Yet it continues to exert its grip on our public administration and on the public mind.

But what are the effects of this mistaken economic picture on public policy? First, a disclaimer. In many ways the embedding of conventional economics within public policy has had a huge positive impact. Indeed it would be impossible to imagine any genuine UK policy discussion today without it. Compared to 30 years ago, there has been a transformation in the understanding of economics within government. It is no longer the main preserve of the Treasury, but also is widely shared within spending departments, quangos and local government. The public economic statistics are far more comprehensive and transparent than they were. And the disciplines which sound economic management implies—of value for money, assessment of costs and benefits and the relative value of money now and in the future—are of huge importance.

Moreover, our target is not just the overall theory, but the panoply of current conventional economics and tools and the very confident approach to government which it carries with it. It is far from easy to separate out economic ideas from political ideology or implementation. But part of our argument is precisely that there has been an unholy alliance between conventional economics and recent (mainly but not exclusively Labour) political ideology, and to explore why this should be. So this mixing-up is to be expected.

Centralisation and Control

Nevertheless, there is real cause for concern. The first point is that this standard economics is not politically neutral. Economists like to think that their discipline is just a tool, to be used in assessing all and any policy regardless of political coloration. But in fact this is not true. As we have seen, this view has no place for people, place and time. It assumes institutions do not exist. It specifically excludes all the paraphernalia and messy human relationships that make up civil society. When conventional economics is applied to policy, there are only two kinds of thing in its models: individual economic agents and the state. And among economic agents, the marginal ones matter more to policy-makers than those at the core—as the case of tax credits has already illustrated.

The effect of this is to build in an unrecognised presumption in favour of centralisation, a top-down command-and-control mentality, and an obsession with interest-group politics at the expense of genuine leadership—precisely the approach to policy-making increasingly adopted by British government over the past two decades. To be sure, the Thatcher government had a certain tolerance for centralisation and impatience with existing public institutions, as we have seen. But it was operating, quite properly, broadly within the existing framework of cabinet government. What is so striking is how the situation has deteriorated under New Labour since 1997. By contrast, the Big Society involves a willingness by central government to alienate power, and to accept that it cannot and should not intervene in every issue that presents itself on the doorstep.

In his famous book *The Anatomy of Britain* Anthony Sampson noted that there was no single centre of power in Britain: rather, power was exercised through a network of institutions including parliament, the judiciary, the crown, the armed forces, the church, the media and the professions. But in conventional economics, as we have noted, there are no institutions as such at all. There are simply economic agents and the state. After 1997 Labour made a fairly systematic attempt to conform government to this pattern, and to disable alternative sources of power, as Peter Oborne and others have described. The result is that the state, and specifically Downing Street and the Treasury, have been more dominant in relative terms during the past decade than at any time in modern memory. But, crucially, they have been tacitly assisted in this task by some of our deepest and most widely shared intellectual preconceptions about the basis of policy itself.

Wrong Operational Model

This conventional economic worldview not only fuels a political tendency to centralisation and control. It also reinforces a bad operational model in government.

To understand the model, one must understand the problem it is designed to solve. As we have seen, services are progressively becoming more expensive, and more expensive relative to manufacturing. The manufacturing sector has massively systematised and proceduralised its operations. The service sector has not, because services offer relatively little scope for productivity gains. This is Baumol's cost disease. The British state is a gigantic provider of public services, including the NHS and the education and welfare systems. So the effect of rising service costs, even before the impact of any waste and inefficiency, is to place unrelenting upward pressure on budgets and so on public spending. More and more money is needed to achieve the same outcomes.

Under Blair and Brown, the response of government was to postpone the problem by spending massively more. But they also recruited a gigantic client state of consultants. These have tried to apply the supposed lessons of lean manufacturing to government in a coercive and standardised way, by creating so-called "public service factories". On this approach, services are specified from the centre; and departments split into front- and back-office functions, given targets, and made subject to inspection and compliance regimes. A focus on people is replaced by a focus on procedures. A silo mentality replaces a holistic view of a given public service as such. Trust is replaced by mistrust. A mania for quantification and cost control infuses the whole. And crucially, real demand for public services is over-shadowed by what systems theorists call "failure demand"—the demands placed on an organisation by people whom it has failed to satisfy.

This approach is founded not merely on political ideology, but on *rigor mortis* economics. In particular, it is founded on two specific ideas that are especially questionable in the context of the public services: that economies of scale are readily achievable, and that private sector economic incentives, and in particular performance-related pay, can be made to work equally well in public service organisations. Neither claim is true. Many studies have shown that performance-related pay actually undermines productivity in many contexts, and especially in public service organisations. Moreover, the economic efficiency of such organisations does not lie merely in having low unit costs. In effect, "public service factories" buy low unit costs by creating huge additional costs, unfulfilled demand and social frustration elsewhere. Just ask anyone who has tried to ring a benefits helpline.

In recent years we have seen the same story played out again and again across the public sector, with a one-size-fits-all approach which ignores the nature of the institutions involved and treats public employees like cattle. The results are higher costs, lower morale and poorer services.

Misleading Rhetoric

Conventional economics, thus, predisposes us in the wrong ways both in the formation and in the implementation of policy. But its highly technical nature also requires it to be handled with extreme care. If not, it offers huge scope for manipulation. It is frequently used not to provide independent grounds for a decision but as a rhetorical means to persuade others of a decision that has already been taken for other reasons. The result is to diminish normal political processes of deliberation and accountability, and often to harm those who cannot afford the necessary external expertise.

Take cost-benefit analysis, for example. In the 1980s this was generally used as a specific tool to appraise relatively small projects which had ascertainable local effects. But this limited use has expanded massively since then to include huge issues and projects in which it is all but impossible to measure the relevant costs and benefits adequately. Even where these can be assessed in some way, it may be impossible to place a cash value on them, as the theory requires. And even when those involved agree that the relevant costs and benefits can be valued in cash terms, that value may prove to be infinite. The person who has lived all their life in the same house or worshipped in the same church, for example, may simply not wish to change under any circumstances. Yet a cost-benefit analysis with infinite costs cannot get started.

And there is a more subtle problem. Cost-benefit analysis normally assesses gains in terms of what those affected would be willing to pay to obtain them; and it analyses losses in terms of what payment those affected would be willing to accept to suffer them. This is partly for reasons of fairness: the idea is that the people who enjoy the gains and suffer the losses are the best judges of how much the gains or losses are worth.

But only rarely do the amounts gainers are willing to pay and losers to accept equal each other. Almost invariably, they do not. What then? Ultimately, one side must be preferred for the analysis to take place at all. And which one is chosen is not a neutral matter. Imagine the government is deadlocked with local green protesters over a new building project. If the question is what the protesters would be willing to pay to avoid damage to the local environment, this implicitly assumes a bias to development. It transforms rights that people used to enjoy into privileges for which they must pay. Conversely, if the question is what the protestors would accept to allow the development to proceed, then given people's known general preference for the status quo, this creates an implicit bias against development. In other words, lying within these abstruse and technical matters are assumptions which can often fundamentally change the basic terms of debate, and unconsciously influence the outcome.

Until relatively recently, the Treasury's *Green Book* only used the willingness-to-pay approach. It therefore carried with it an implicit bias in favour of development. But this, though important, is incidental. The wider point is that cost-benefit analysis and other formal mathematical tools are of far less value than currently believed, and seriously prone to abuse. Their value is often more rhetorical than real.

Bias Against Risk

The fourth and final effect concerns risk. Risk is always present in human society. We have already seen how it is often misjudged by individuals. But it is also very poorly understood by government. The result is that we have worse government and less joyful lives. Why should this be?

Britain has a single model of the state, broadly speaking, and a uniform and top-down process of policymaking which suppresses variety, experimentation and local innovation. The result is that this country almost certainly has a huge long-term exposure to unnecessary or unwanted risk. One or two areas apart, moreover, there is little evidence to suggest that the British government has made any systematic attempt to measure or manage risk. Indeed its recent corporatism and authoritarianism have only increased the problem.

Moreover, government itself has an embedded aversion to risk. Nothing succeeds like success—except in the civil service, where success comes a poor second to not being seen to fail. There are good reasons for this, including a dedication to procedure, a desire to preserve public money and awareness of the ever-present scrutiny of politicians. But the inability to tolerate failure causes government to over-invest in error, rather than acknowledge it; and it prevents the open assessment of failures when they occur, until the individual responsible moves on and failure becomes someone else's problem.

In the case of individuals, we can think of risk as the possibility of gain or loss. People take risks in part because they want the gains that risk can bring: they drive fast in order to get somewhere quicker, they take drugs to get high, they go rock-climbing for the thrill of it. Occasionally, of course, they get the losses that come from risk and not the gains. But taking risks is not irrational. On the contrary, it appears to be both rational and an inevitable part of human nature.

Indeed, the evidence suggests that we each have a "risk thermostat"; that is, a default setting towards a certain level of risk. The setting will differ between people, and across a lifetime. But it adjusts to suit the circumstances. If we are taking too little risk, we naturally tend to adjust our risk-taking upwards. If too much, we tend to reduce it. Thus one of the unexpected consequences of the seatbelt laws has been to raise the speed at which cars are driven. Why? Because seat belts reduce the risk of serious accident. So drivers can go faster without any net increase in risk.

Now consider the matter from a public perspective. Accidents show up in the economic models as losses. But there is generally no quantification in cost-benefit analysis of the reward arising from any risks taken. Furthermore, as the state is extended into private life, the possibility increases that some public authority will be held responsible for an accident and attract criticism or, increasingly, litigation. The effect of this is that the state always seeks not to manage risk in society, but to reduce it.

But risk has rewards as well as penalties. So the inevitable result is a ratchet which pushes us towards bossy government, higher costs, greater paperwork and less joy. These effects are everywhere to see, in schools with over-engineered playgrounds but no new books; in an intrusive culture of official health-and-safety jobsworths; or memorably in the 2008 ban on undergraduates at Anglia Ruskin University from tossing their mortarboards in the air on graduation day, for fear of the safety consequences.

And there is also huge social frustration. The desire to manage away risk undermines the possibility of achievement. No amount of words designed to lift a young man's self-esteem will substitute for conquering a fear, taking a risk and succeeding. But a person who is unable to take their default level of risk in one way will find other ways to do so, and a society which is systematically prevented from taking its desired level of risk will find itself deeply thwarted and unhappy. Yet this is what seems to have been happening in Britain in recent years.

It may seem fanciful to connect such things as the recent rise in drug abuse and knife crime with the social acceptance of a standard economic worldview. But the present line of thought suggests a clear linkage. Intriguingly, it also suggests that policies which increase the scope for human self-expression and risk-taking will reduce social frustration and increase well-being.

Looking Ahead

The world of textbook economics is perfect in itself, but importantly flawed as a tool of policy. As we have seen, it is static. It excludes precisely the things that make society flourish: people, institutions, culture. Its prestige and technical difficulty make it hard to question. However, the conventional approach is far from being a neutral tool of policy. On the contrary, it silently carries with it several damaging biases: towards centralisation in government; towards a flawed operational model for provision of public services; and against the natural human instinct to take risks. And finally, it constrains the very possibility of debate as to the kind of economic future we want to have, at precisely the moment we need that debate.

But all is not lost. There are other tools in the toolbox, other ideas we can consider. In particular, imperfect information opens the door to new ideas. If markets not only can but must operate on imperfect information, then we have no reason to think that the textbook model is perfectly efficient. But if that is true, then we have no reason to prefer only a maximally libertarian economy. The way is clear for a more nuanced debate as to what varieties of capitalism there are, and which of them we wish to move towards.

Unfortunately, our political system has not of late been up to such a debate. It has been caught up in poll-driven positioning or party ideology. And it has lacked the conceptual framework in which to discuss the social, cultural and economic issues at the heart of the Big Society. To these we now turn.

5 **Left and Right**

> Why cannot the leaders of the Labour party face the fact that they are not sectaries of an outworn creed, mumbling moss-grown demi-semi Fabian Marxism; but the heirs of eternal Liberalism?
>
> *John Maynard Keynes, 1939 article in* **The New Statesman**

As so often, Keynes saw further than his contemporaries. We might ask two questions: when more of the state isn't the solution, and conventional economics is dead, then where is politics to go? And: what principles should inspire and direct reflection on politics and policy?

So far our focus has been on economics and society. We have looked at the underlying condition of the British economy and of British society, and traced many of our current problems to the long-term growth and centralization of the state. And we have suggested an underlying set of causes: a misunderstanding of economics within government, and an increasingly economic and financial view of human nature within wider society. The point is not to be unduly pessimistic or partisan, but clear-eyed about what will be needed to improve our public services, and the society that they serve.

The idea of the Big Society is at root a response to the two questions above, and the next few chapters examine what it amounts to, the different traditions from which it springs, and its core philosophical justification. But first we need to look a little deeper at the anatomy of British politics itself.

Post-Democratic Politics

Over the past twenty years the nature of our politics has fundamentally changed. We live now in an age not of "push" but of "pull" politics, a politics not of conviction and ideology but of voter segmentation and control. It is consumer- and not producer-led, based more and more on personality than on policy, more on "narrative" than facts. With a few glorious exceptions, it does not select politicians with clear ideas who can convince others to follow them, and who are self-confident enough to accept blame for mistakes. Rather, it selects politicians who can make themselves distinctive in the media, who tend to cater to electors rather than lead them, and who believe—with some reason—that any admission of error, uncertainty or frailty is likely to be terminal.

In such circumstances, the tendency towards "ice cream van" politics is reinforced. Each party tries to corner as much of the electoral marketplace as possible by moving into the centre. Under Tony Blair, New Labour succeeded in occupying this centre ground. It did so by jettisoning previous ideological commitments; by homogenising and centralising the party organisation and suppressing internal disagreement; and by a systematic, unprecedented and constitutionally suspect attempt to manage and control the media. Thus has the art of politics finally supplanted the art of government.

So much is well documented. This cynical and narrow view has even been given a name: post-democratic politics. But some of its implications have not been fully understood. The first is to confer increased power on an incumbent government, and so to lengthen its "normal" lifetime. Incumbency always confers some political advantage; this is magnified when 24-hour media coverage has shortened individual and institutional memory, and when government controls a huge flow of news stories about itself.

But post-democratic politics does not merely reduce the likelihood of a change of government; it also threatens to undermine its popular basis altogether. If an incumbent government always knows what you the voter say you want, if its policies are regularly changing in ways that fit the perceived majority public opinion and that do not respect previous ideological boundaries, if its personalities are regularly refreshed to meet the recurrent desire for change, and if popular political memory is selective and foreshortened, then—in theory at least—why vote for anyone else? The effect is to give to British government a Maoist ethos of continuous revolution, and to sustain the dominance of presentation over ideas.

Such a politics is easy to criticise, but difficult to cure. After all, in other areas of life those who meet our stated needs tend to be rewarded. Over the longer term its results are to increase political volatility, to push public attention to fringe parties who can make wild promises safe in the knowledge that they will not be held responsible for them, and to stoke popular distrust with politicians.

Yet even our politics today is not what it was in 1997—it has moved on. We are more media-aware and more savvy about spin. What matter now are authenticity and legitimacy. Authenticity: is this person who they claim to be? Is this a real person, or a mouthpiece?

And legitimacy: do they have the right to say what they say? Do they really, by background or experience or commitment, know what they're talking about? Few of us could meet such standards fully; and few politicians, from whom we constantly demand quick answers rather than thoughtful ones. But nevertheless our desire is rightly to trust, and trust remains the grail of post-democratic politics.

The Fabian Takeover

Trust is at a premium in part because popular belief in the value of our political system and political leaders has rarely been lower. To this can be added a growing popular sense of the limitations both of the state and of conventional economics. Where, then, can we turn for some firm ground on which to stand? Where can we find a principled, long-term vision of social renewal?

One thing is clear: not on the left, as it is presently constituted. It has been extremely tempting for journalists and politicians to regard the 2010 election as an unfortunate aberration, rather than as a sign of anything more fundamentally wrong. After all, the Prime Minister was known to be personally unpopular, many voters remained alienated by the Iraq war, the country was in a deep recession, and the eventual electoral outcome was not as bad for Labour as many on the left had previously feared.

The creation of the first Coalition government in the UK for 65 years has encouraged these views: for how stable could a coalition be, especially in the face of economic crisis? With a new leader in place, a huge fiscal consolidation under way and the poll returns improving, the electoral pendulum must surely swing back fairly soon. All that was needed, it was said, was time and a measure of party unity.

Of course nothing is predictable in politics. Swing the pendulum may, and quickly. But this complacent view is a huge trap for the left. For the truth is that the Labour party is in deep crisis. This is not just because Labour is a sect, in former cabinet minister James Purnell's words, which has lost the ability to communicate with voters: it is because it has nothing authentic at present to communicate. Streams of arm-waving press releases are not a substitute for genuine vision. Complacency about a rapid return to government is not a substitute for thorough self-examination.

But understanding the real nature of this crisis requires us to step back a little. Historically, the left has always reflected many distinct and overlapping strands: non-conformist traditions of religious, cultural and political dissent; working class traditions (often thoroughly small-c conservative) of self-help; the trades union movement; many varieties of Marxism and Communism; and Fabianism.

Fabianism was the product of the Fabian Society, which was founded in 1884 with the aim of establishing socialist reform of British politics and life. The Society was distinctive in rejecting the revolutionary politics of the extreme left. Instead it adopted a gradualist approach, taking its name from Fabius Cunctator, the "delayer" who conquered Hannibal in the Punic Wars by harrying him and always avoiding outright confrontation. From early on the Society was led by the formidable team of Sidney and Beatrice Webb, and the Webbs gathered around themselves a group of well-known intellectuals including GB Shaw, HG Wells, the Woolfs, the economist Graham Wallas and, for a time, Bertrand Russell. These were followed between the wars by such Labour intellectuals as GDH Cole, Harold Laski and RH Tawney.

Fabianism thus stood in strong contrast to other traditions on the left. It was overwhelmingly middle class, mainly based in the South, and dominated not by preachers, radicals, shopkeepers or union organisers but by intellectuals. It had a strong belief in making new policy; specifically, its thinkers were preoccupied with applying enlightenment ideas, and in particular the findings of modern science, to British society. They quickly discovered that the perfect vehicle through which to apply these ideas, and ensure their own continued indispensability and prestige, was the expanding apparatus of the state. In effect, they saw the state as a beneficent force by which the many imperfections of human nature and human society could be eliminated through science. There followed a huge array of policy proposals ranging from a national minimum wage and a universal health service to nationalisation of land and slum clearance—and not excluding a persistent interest in eugenics and selective breeding.

During the course of the 20th Century, Fabianism defeated its challengers and took control of the left: in the first decades intellectually and then—assisted by the collective experience of the Second World War—politically. Every Labour Prime Minister has been a Fabian. Other traditions on the left, such as those of non-conformist dissent, guild socialism and working-class self-help, have been sidestepped and subsumed. As the Liberal coalition split under Asquith and Lloyd George, Labour was able to step in and take over. When Attlee's government was overwhelmingly elected in 1945, this seemed to many to be the final validation of Fabian state socialism in the UK.

It is sometimes forgotten that the result has been a disaster for the political left. As David Marquand has pointed out, in the fifty years after 1868 the old two party system of Conservatives vs. Liberals produced 27 years of Conservative or Conservative-dominated government, as against 23 years for the Liberals, for a 54%-46% split. Since Labour became the official party of opposition in 1922, the ensuing 88 years have split 55 Conservative or Conservative-dominated government vs. 33 for Labour, or a 62.5%-37.5% split. In other words, the advent of Labour has cost the British political left more than seven whole years in government since 1922. Those seven missing years are longer than every Labour government bar one.

The Fabian takeover created Labour's deep-dyed commitment to state expansion and centralisation of public services. But that takeover has also had implications for the party itself. It has tended to reinforce the party's self-identification in tribal terms as the promoter of a class interest rather than a wider vision of human values which could appeal to all sections of the populace. It has thus inhibited the formation of a wider coalition of the left of the kind seen within the Democratic party in the US, and in many European countries.

The ironies are manifest. For one of the earliest and most telling analyses was offered by no less a figure than Leon Trotsky. Trotsky's 1925 book *Where Is Britain Going?* was one of the first to point out that Fabianism was not an attempt to empower the ordinary working people of this country, but an attempt to suppress them. In his words "Throughout the whole history of the British Labour movement there has been pressure by the bourgeoisie upon the proletariat through the agency of radicals, intellectuals, drawing-room and church socialists and Owenites who reject the class struggle and advocate the principle of social solidarity, preach collaboration with the bourgeoisie, bridle, enfeeble and politically debase the proletariat."

So, in many ways, it has proved. The 20th Century is replete with the demise of highly effective working-class institutions which fell by the wayside as the state took over their functions. And where are the great dissenters within the Labour party now? The deeper issue thus goes far beyond an acknowledgement that New Labour has become too much of a sect. It goes far beyond the narrow choice, inexperience and evident limitations of the candidates in its recent leadership election. It is about the very point and purpose of the left as such—where it has come from, what it stands for, and why.

Tory Pragmatism

Something similar might have been said of the Conservatives in 1997. But there has been a huge difference here between left and right: the right has had a far wider range of traditions on which it can draw to renew itself. It has never become a sect.

Indeed, it has almost been too inclusive. For as a body of political thought Conservatism is all but impossible to define. The career of Benjamin Disraeli illustrates the point perfectly. The young Disraeli opposed social reform, for the sound conservative reasons that it eroded property rights and local independence while increasing taxation and regulation. Thus he voted against cheap bread in 1846, against the Public Health Act of 1848, against the Mining Act of 1850, and against the General Board of Health Act in 1854. He opposed the Privy Council's idea in 1839 to give the Committee in Council on Education £30,000 to spend on educating the English poor, so much did he fear the intrusiveness of state inspection of schools.

The older Disraeli, on the other hand, led social reform as Prime Minister for the sound conservative reasons that it relieved poverty, squalor and hardship, and promoted social cohesion, or "One Nation" as we have come to call it. He won the 1874 general election by pitching the Tories as the party of real reform against a Liberal cabinet which he derided as "a range of exhausted volcanoes". He spent the next two years passing eleven major acts of social reform across a number of areas, including trade union rights, factory conditions, public health, education and housing. During this legislative flood the condition of the people, rather than the interests of the landed, became the central preoccupation of the Tory party.

Just the kind of unscrupulous U-turn to be expected of Conservatives in general, it might be argued, and of Disraeli in particular. Haven't the Tories always been political magpies, picking and choosing between ideas to suit the moment, ruthlessly appropriating their opponents' most popular themes, and discarding hitherto fervent beliefs once they cease to be expedient?

It is easy to deride Tory statecraft as the subjugation of abstract principle to the practical goal of winning and maintaining power. It may be lauded as flexibility or condemned as cynicism, but it must be recognised as indispensable to the popularity of conservatism as a political creed. It was not by accident that the Conservative party spent two-thirds of the 20th century in government. Disraeli himself cited the enfranchisement of the industrial working class as a strategic imperative to support social reform. Had he not been heeded, the Tories might have gone the way of the Liberals.

However, this is only half the picture. A further look would show that this tension between principles is intrinsic to conservatism itself. Not only that, it is a crucial reason why conservatism has been so extraordinarily successful over the years as a political movement. The Tories' habitual switching between different strands of ideas is not merely the product of electoral calculation. Rather, it reflects genuine philosophical tensions within conservatism as a body of thought. The

Conservatives have been a "broad church" in electoral appeal precisely because they have been a broad church in ideas. Thus, to take only a few examples, conservatives have called for greater social cohesion, but also for individual freedom. For free trade, but also for protectionism. For imperialism, but also for isolationism. For central standards and efficiency in government, but also for local independence from White-hall. For the relief of poverty, but also for lower taxes. For stronger links to Europe, and for weaker ones.

Two Traditions

Historically, in Great Britain these principles have clustered around two rival traditions: a liberal or libertarian conservatism concerned with free markets, localism and private property, and a paternalist conservatism that has prioritised community and social stability.

Of these, the latter has been more prominent over the past two centuries. Indeed Conservatives were legislating for trade union rights a generation before the Labour party was founded, and establishing public health projects before Aneurin Bevan was born. Disraeli's last ministry represents a 19th Century high watermark of Tory paternalism, while the Macmillan government, whose "middle way" entrenched and expanded the welfare state forty years before Blair's "Third Way", represented such a mark for the 20th. By contrast Thatcherism was something of a throwback to Gladstonian liberalism, with its rolling back of the state, its moral fervour and its emphasis on individual freedom.

Often, however, there has been stalemate between these traditions. From the arguments over social reform in the mid-19th century, to the defections over free trade in the early-20th century, to the "wet" resistance to the New Right in the 1970s, to the current debates about tax cuts and academic selection, British conservatism has had contradictory instincts on public policy and the role of the state: one urging greater scope for individual initiative, the other more reconciled to large and active government. That both these contrasting principles can legitimately claim to belong to the conservative intellectual tradition is precisely what makes such stalemates so agonising.

It is also a peculiarly British problem, as centre-right parties in most Western democracies have chosen one way or the other between the two traditions. The mainstream conservative parties of Europe, such as Germany's Christian Democratic Union and France's Gaullist party, are essentially comfortable with a paternalist view of the state as an agent of social change and the embodiment of the nation. Europe's decade-long affliction with low growth and high unemployment has pushed these parties in a reformist direction. But the most far-reaching proposals for economic liberalisation still come from smaller liberal parties hoping to find their way into a coalition government.

By contrast, to simplify still more grossly, centre-right parties in the Anglo-Saxon world, namely the US Republicans and the Australian Liberals, have traditionally espoused an essentially liberal brand of conservatism. They have emphasised self-reliance and voluntarism over benign big government, most recently of course in America with a strongly Christian backdrop. With the important exception of Ronald Reagan's presidency, the Grand Old Party's flirtation with fiscal profligacy under George W. Bush represents an aberration from the mainstream of American conservative thought. It was not until the Eisenhower Republicanism of the 1950s that the American right reconciled itself to Franklin Roosevelt's New Deal reforms, and it has taken all of 40 years for it to accept the permanence of Great Society programmes such as Medicare. The neo-liberal triumphs of the Clinton years, such as welfare reform, the balanced budget resolution and the absolute cut in federal payroll, were all conservative ideas forced by a Republican Congress on a reluctant Democrat President. Only on national defence, and on hot-button cultural issues such as abortion, have American conservatives consistently envisaged a role for a large and active state.

Another curiosity is that the two traditions of conservative thought seem to switch sides when the debate shifts from economics and public services to the legal and moral issues of nationhood, criminal justice and foreign policy. Here, it has been those on the liberal or libertarian side who have appreciated the utility of the state as a "bully pulpit" from which to cultivate patriotism against what is seen as a dangerously rootless post-modernity; who tend towards a more aggressive posture on law and order; and who are more willing to employ the armed forces in the pursuit of British interests abroad.

Conversely, it has been those on the paternalist side who have been sceptical of both the principle and possibility of a state-led civic nationalism, who are mistrustful of state expansionism and centralisation in criminal justice, and who have preferred cautious, stability-maximising realism in foreign policy. This again serves to illuminate the complexity and heterogeneity of conservative thought.

Context and Instinct

As in the political arena, so in the intellectual. Conservatives do no less thinking than liberals or socialists. The difference is that they have never settled on a conclusion. Conservatism is in effect a cluster of ideas competing with each other for market share. Which of the two traditions holds sway in any given situation depends on nothing more high-minded than the circumstances that obtain at the time. Context is crucial. The practical conditions of the here and now guide conservatives as surely as pre-written doctrines guide socialists and utilitarian liberals. A political conservative must determine the requirements of a particular situation, and reflect on which of his or her principles are to be deployed and how.

This may require a shift from one principle to another over time, or the simultaneous application of different principles to different situations. Each of these may be disdained as hypocrisy, and of course sometimes they may actually be hypocritical. But politics is not logic. Absolute consistency in the application of abstract principle to practical politics is rarely possible and never wise. The British electorate, with its preference for common sense over grand theory, usually rewards this insight at elections, even as it abuses it between them.

What ultimately distinguishes conservatism from its rival creeds, therefore, is not so much the views it holds, though some of these are unique to conservatism, as the way it holds them. Socialism and liberalism are, at root, theories and ideologies: fundamental interpretations of the nature of history and of "the good", from which policy programmes are supposedly inferred. Conservatism is no such thing. It is instinctive, not theoretical; a disposition, not a doctrine; realistic and sceptical, not grandiose or utopian; accepting of the imperfectability of man, not restless to overcome it; and anxious to improve the lot of the many not by referring to some plan, but by working with the grain of what Kant called "the crooked timber of humanity". It is precisely its reluctance to accord sacred status to any abstract idea that allows conservatism to incorporate so many of them. It is precisely its refusal to regard change as a good in itself that makes it so well qualified to manage change most prudently.

All well and good, one might think. But where does the Big Society fit in? It seems to fall under neither of these traditions. David Cameron has often remarked that "There is such a thing as society". But that seems to imply that society is something over and above individual people, which hardly places it within the Conservatives' libertarian tradition. On the other hand the follow-up "... it's just not the same thing as the State" hardly suggests a new Tory paternalism. So what is the Big Society, and where does it come from? To this question we now turn.

6 **The Foundations of Society**

Any man's death diminishes me, because I am involved in mankind. And therefore never send to know for whom the bell tolls. It tolls for thee.
John Donne

The more [the state] stands in the place of associations, the more will individuals, losing the notion of combining together, require its assistance. These are cause and effect that unceasingly create each other.
Alexis de Tocqueville

To adapt a celebrated motion on the monarchy of 1780 in the House of Commons, the power of the state has grown, is growing, and ought to be diminished. But where can we find a coherent, positive, humane and long-term view of how our society can be improved, independently of the state? To see such a vision, we need to dig down, briefly, to philosophical bedrock: to Thomas Hobbes, and to Michael Oakeshott. At this point the argument briefly gets a bit more theoretical.

Our basic theory of the state derives largely from Hobbes. Hobbes was born in 1588, his birth reputedly brought on by his mother's alarm at news of the Spanish Armada, and he died in 1679 at the age of 91. He thus spent his youth in the era of Shakespeare, Jonson and Donne; his middle age during the constitutional crises of the 1630s, from which he fled to Paris in 1640 just in time to escape the English Civil War; and his old age in the midst of a scientific revolution that, inspired by the insights of Galileo, Descartes and Newton, continues to this day.

Hobbes was employed throughout most of his adult life as tutor to the Cavendish family, that of the Earls (and later Dukes) of Devonshire; and while in Paris he also acted as tutor to Charles, Prince of Wales. Yet despite, or rather because of, this background, he did not shrink from addressing the basic philosophical question: on what legitimate basis does government exercise its powers? Or to put it another way: by what right does the state exist?

In his book *Leviathan*, published in 1651, Hobbes argued that human government owed its existence to a contract between all members of society, by which they voluntarily traded autonomy for security. In the absence of government people lived in a state of nature, a "war of all against all", in which all were constantly at risk and constantly afraid of violent death; a state in which people's lives were, in his famous phrase, "solitary, poor, nasty, brutish and short". The social contract is simply a rational response to this fear. Individuals cede some freedoms on a once-and-for-all basis to a single sovereign authority which, by guaranteeing civil order and secure borders, gives them the space and the legal and physical protection to associate freely with each other.

It is this act of empowerment that makes society possible. The sovereign authority may in principle be a single person, a group of persons, or indeed the people themselves. It may be a monarchy, an oligarchy or a democracy. But it and it alone is the source of legitimate power, and its legitimacy derives from being freely given by all. The sovereign can properly pass legislation because we, the people, have authorised it to do so; and according to Hobbes we are under a moral obligation, not merely a legal obligation, to obey its laws for the same reason.

Hobbes's genius lies in providing an account of sovereignty that locates its authority in the voluntary choices of individuals, not in an act of God or in some dubious and ill-defined collective will. His account is so familiar as to be the common currency of practical politics even today. Of course, few if any nowadays would follow Hobbes in his more extreme views: in seeing the sovereign as absolutely powerful, or the people as giving up all their freedoms to the sovereign through the social contract. But nevertheless it seems that many people, including those who have neither read Hobbes nor even know his name, possess an instinctively Hobbesian conception of political authority, grounding it in rational self-protection, rather than in any divine bequest.

Yet its very familiarity has blinded us to its consequences. For what is this contract? Not a description of any historical event, but an idealisation of a legal relationship between the individual and the state. The formal beauty of this idealisation is that it makes no assumptions as to human motivation or interests, beyond assuming that all are solely motivated by the fear of violent death. It is thus the intellectual precursor of the economic models of today, in which people are treated as though they are purely self-interested seekers of profit or some other form of "utility"; as individual atoms cut off from each other, who react positively to opportunities for gain and negatively to the possibility of loss.

Hobbes, in effect, does something similar. For him, humankind is not innately bad, but people naturally desire freedom for themselves and control over others; they are, in his words, continually in competition for honour and dignity. It is these desires that, unfettered, render the state of nature so abhorrent. But it is specifically the fear of violent death that motivates the social contract. This is a minimal basis for the existence of the state.

In defining the state, therefore, and in order to define it, Hobbes has defined the individual as well: the two are point and counterpoint to each other, the two basic elements from which his politics is derived. But if we reverse the image, so to speak, and ask not what is included but what is left out, what do we find?

What we find is that Hobbes makes three crucial omissions, which still set the terms for current arguments about state and society today. First, he deliberately ignores, as we have seen, the astonishing richness and diversity of human emotions, aspirations, interests and goals.

Secondly, in his extreme individualism, in seeking to rule out any such thing as "the people", or the "common will" as such, over and above actual individuals themselves, Hobbes deliberately ignores all intermediate institutions between the individual and the state. The family, the church, the club or guild—and today, the union, the company or the team—are secondary entities, created by individuals once they have achieved the protections of the social contract. Civil laws are, in his words, but chains from the lips of the sovereign to men's ears—with nothing in between.

Finally, Hobbes builds in a moral presumption in favour of the state and against the individual. After all, the social contract is freely entered into by us; indeed the sovereign state just is us, to the extent that it represents our pooled and delegated authority. According to him, we cannot demur or grumble, therefore, when our authorised sovereign acts in ways of which we do not approve, except when it threatens our survival. We have freely empowered it, and if it acts contrary to our interests, then tough luck. There can in general be no conscientious objection or civil disobedience in Hobbes's state.

Like the social contract itself, these omissions cast a very long intellectual shadow. Indeed they still structure present debates over the nature of the state and the political alternatives available to us. We shall come back to them in due course. For now, the key point is that the social contract à la Hobbes is designed to explain the rightful existence, authority and legitimacy of the state, but at root it says nothing whatever about society, or the relationship between state and society. We may know that the sovereign authority is authorised to pass laws, and that individuals are obliged, and can be properly compelled, to obey them. We may know that the social contract is what allows society as such to come into existence at all. But we know nothing more. We have an outline, but none of the fine detail or colour.

But unless we understand the two notions of state and society better, we have no chance of seeing what is at stake here: what, if anything, we are giving up by allowing the state to grow continuously, or what an alternative vision of our society might be.

The Essential Tension

For this, we need Michael Oakeshott. Oakeshott's was the pattern of an outwardly uneventful academic life. He was born in 1901, and died in 1990. He studied at Cambridge, and then taught there, at Oxford and at the London School of Economics. During his long lifetime, he published two books of essays and two monographs, each of the latter in its own way a masterpiece—and each sufficiently rigorous and unfashionable in viewpoint as to fall, like Hume's *Treatise*, still-born from the press. He is little known and less read today. He lacked any formal academic qualification in philosophy. But he has rightly been called the greatest British political philosopher since Edmund Burke.

Oakeshott's thought ranges far more widely than in politics. But what we need here is the distinction that he draws between two kinds of society: between civil society and enterprise society. A civil society is an association of citizens, individuals who are formally equal in their rights before the law. As citizens, they have something in common with each other. But this is not a common goal, or purpose, or plan. Rather, it is just that they recognise that they are all bound, one no more and no less than any other, by a system of laws, and that these laws derive from a single civil authority.

An enterprise society is very different. It is one in which the whole of society itself is organised as a communal enterprise or undertaking in its own right. In this case, individuals are not viewed as citizens, endowed with certain basic rights and protections. Rather, they are seen as contributors to a common project, who come together to achieve a recognised goal or goals. These goals may be economic, such as greater national prosperity or industrial productivity. But they need not be. They may be cultural, ethnic or religious goals, such as cultural unity, ethnic purity or religious orthodoxy. An enterprise society thus has nothing as such to do with business or "enterprise" in that sense. On the contrary, its overarching purpose may be entirely different.

As one might expect, these different types of society operate in very different ways. In a civil society, the rules will generally be procedural, not substantive; they will set frameworks within which people can live, not targets for them to achieve. They will be universal not specific, applying to all and not identifying certain subgroups of citizens for gain or penalty. And they will say what all citizens must do as a matter of obedience to the law, not in virtue of a commitment to engineer certain social outcomes. In a civil society, thus, the function of government is not to do anything as such—it is just to govern. The state has no goals or projects of its own, over and above those of the individuals or groups being governed. Instead, its role is to devise, promulgate and enforce laws by which people may go about their private business in an orderly and secure way.

In an enterprise society, on the other hand, the function of government is precisely to achieve certain social objectives. It can never be content merely to govern. It is, as it were, ambitious. The laws it creates will tend to set specific goals, to assume the state's right to manage people, to treat people as a means to achieve the state's own priorities. Government in an enterprise society can never rest easy, for nothing is ever as good as it could be, and so there will always appear to be scope for state intervention to improve it. If poverty or economic underperformance or crime exists, it is but a short step for the nanny state to take upon itself the task of improving the situation.

We can readily see both conceptions at work in British history: the notion of civil society in such things as Magna Carta, legal due process and voting rules; and that of enterprise society in Great Britain PLC, the No. 10 Downing Street "Delivery Unit", five year plans, public service targets, and the national bid to host the Olympic Games in London.

Oakeshott's two conceptions of society are idealised, of course. Neither is, nor ever could be, exemplified in its pure form, and so every actual society has elements or aspects of each. The two are, however, distinct, indeed formally exclusive of each other: philosophically, one is organised under the category of procedure, the other under that of purpose. In short, they are rivals, struggling over the soul of a given society, forever pulling it in the directions of self-restraint or ambition as each gains or loses the upper hand, in an essential tension.

So much for the theory. Why does this distinction matter? The first thing is to note that the 20th century was the century of the enterprise society. State provision of goods and services in the name of common social goals grew rapidly in every major industrialised country around the world. Of course, those in authority have never been indifferent to people's economic or social well-being, on pain of unrest, loss of office or revolution. But for the state itself to be used as economic engine, safety net or service provider has been a modern, and specifically a 20th century, innovation.

We have already seen how this occurred in the UK. But it is important to acknowledge that the most extreme forms of tyranny in the last century arose from what is, intellectually, the same source. Both communism and fascism have a common root in their desire to organise all of society's resources to achieve a set of "social" goals determined by the state. In communist Russia, officially at least, these goals included the achievement of a "classless society" and the "dictatorship of the proletariat". The chosen means included the expropriation of private property; the nationalisation of agricultural and industrial production; huge programmes of forced industrialisation and collectivisation; the central administration of exports, imports, prices and incomes; and state control over banks and other financial institutions.

In contrast, Nazi Germany preserved much of the form and some of the substance of private property, free markets and democratic institutions. But it too was a ramified enterprise society. Its goals were economic recovery, the achievement of national racial and cultural purity, and ultimately of course the military occupation and control of Europe. Nationalisation was only used selectively. Instead, companies were organised into cartels under administrative boards, allied to banks; the unions were broken and wage controls imposed; there was a huge programme of public works; and an enormous mobilisation and expansion of the armed forces. The story of how Nazi Germany sought to achieve its other goals is too well-known and too awful to need re-telling here.

To many people, each of these very extreme examples of tyranny is a one-off, a unique social phenomenon unlike any other. To find a pattern between them, let alone to link them to processes and events currently at work in modern western democracies, may seem at best poor reasoning, and at worst simply offensive.

Yet they do serve to bring out a more general principle: that the growth of the enterprise society invariably tends to abridge our freedom before the law. Recall that the enterprise view is one that judges people, not as citizens, but by their contribution to some overarching corporate goal. In such a society, the interests of citizens are always subordinate to the overall project, which is invariably determined by the sovereign power, by the state itself. The best citizen is, thus, not a citizen at all, but a star worker, like the famous Russian miner Stakhanov; or a star entrepreneur, or parent, or saver, or taxpayer. Formal equality is thus replaced by a social metric assessing people by their contributions to the corporate whole; and, often, by a strand of public moralising that seeks to justify these assessments.

Fascism is thus the worst case of the enterprise society in action; the case in which all private interests are subordinated to the designated goals of the society itself. We can see this in Mussolini's infamous slogan "Tutto nello Stato, niente al di fuori dello Stato, nulla contra lo Stato" ("everything in the State, nothing outside the State, nothing against the State"). Or take a perhaps still more notorious example, Hitler's "ein Volk, ein Reich, ein Führer" ("one people, one regime, one leader"). This was not merely a call for Germans to associate themselves with a national project incarnated in the leader's own person. It was also a tacit invitation to ignore intermediate institutions or protective laws in so doing.

However, the defects of the enterprise society are not merely accidental, but reflect a deeper incoherence. This is what Oakeshott calls rationalism: the belief that skilled activities like the activity of governing can be reduced to a set of explicit rules or instructions, or that different languages or modes of understanding can be applied willy-nilly to different subjects.

At its most politically extreme, this rationalism can be seen in planned economies and planned societies, which seek to capture and organise the staggeringly diverse potential of human beings, and frame it on some Procrustean bed. But it is not an either/or matter; on the contrary, it operates almost everywhere to greater or lesser degree. Thus it can be seen not merely in the sweeping objections of von Mises and Hayek to the very idea of a planned economy, but in the far more familiar thought that politics merely consists of a series of economic, social or cultural problems to be solved—and in the anguish that follows when those problems turn out to be deeply interrelated and their solutions to have unanticipated consequences.

Rationalism also shapes the minds of its believers. It substitutes a single idea for a messy reality. It dispels sober judgement and replaces it with a sense of certainty. In short, it encourages fundamentalism: a politics of faith over a politics of doubt.

This is a deeply conservative line of thought, pushing us away from ideology and towards scepticism and pragmatic principle. But politically it cuts both ways: it is a devastating intellectual critique of Fabianism, its guiding belief in the state and its conflation of state and society. But it also undermines the economic fundamentalism of free market über-libertarians, who see no role for the state at all. And, as we shall see, it clips the wings of technocrats and ideologues who would reduce all political or social questions to economic ones, or indeed substitute economics for politics as such.

The Idea of a Connected Society

Oakeshott brilliantly illuminates the relation between state and society: the essential tension between the claims of a civil and an enterprise society, the dangers of rationalism, and by implication the costs and benefits of Britain's steady transformation into a more purely enterprise society.

Yet there is a missing category in Oakeshott, which echoes what is missing in Hobbes. Like his predecessor, and for similar reasons, Oakeshott has merely given us a minimal specification. A civil society is based on procedure, a framework of laws between sovereign and citizen, but it is nothing more. An enterprise society is project-based, society conceived as an organised purposeful whole, but it is nothing more. Everything else must be filled in. Each must be given an ecosystem: each must be populated with living, loving and dying human beings who come together in groups or institutions of every imaginable kind.

The omission becomes more telling if we notice that Oakeshott's fundamental categories of procedure and purpose are insufficient to describe some of these institutions. For what kind of association is a family? Or a football supporters' club? Or a company? Of course each obeys certain procedures, and each can have a purpose: bearing and bringing up children, cheering the team on, making profits. But anyone who thought of these institutions solely in such terms would only partly understand them. They would be missing a crucial feature, which helps to explain the centrality of these institutions in our culture. This is that in very different ways they are based in and constituted by human affection.

Readers of Nick Hornby's book *Fever Pitch* will need no reminding of this. For it vividly describes the emotions of the fanatical football supporter: the hero-worship, the dedication required to attend every match, the hatred of competing teams. Yet what sustains the supporter through the seasons, year in, year out? Not some top-down incentive plan; not the rules of the supporter's club; and not even the success of the team—as Newcastle United fans can testify. Surely it is the tribal feeling of belonging, of being inside the circle and part of the group.

If this is right, then we need to recognise a new category, a new kind of association, one based on affection rather than procedure or purpose. In the spirit of Oakeshott, we can call this missing category that of "connected" or philic association, after the Greek word *philia*, a word whose various meanings includes "friendship", "tie", "affection", and "regard". And with it in mind, we can restore what Hobbes has left out: a focus on human lives, and what allows them to flourish; a place between the individual and the state for all those intermediate "sideways" institutions which link us all together and give fulfilment to our lives; a counterbalancing moral presumption in favour of the individual; and a recognition that what motivates human beings needs not merely to be a matter of the stick and the carrot, complying with rules or achieving some collective goal, but of culture, identity and belonging. It is this new category of philic association that lays the philosophical groundwork for modern ideas of social capital, networking and connectivity—and for the Big Society.

So far so good. But it is not enough simply to recognise the possibility of a connected society, or even to describe certain institutions in terms of their linkages, of the human connections that inspire them, or of their place within the social web. We need to specify what a society would be like that was organised horizontally, not vertically, so as to place these intermediate institutions at its heart.

Society and State

But the reader may reasonably be feeling rather sceptical at this point. Where is all this going? Isn't a "connected society" just the kind of debased verbiage which desperate politicos tend to reach for when they have run out of ideas?

No. It would be a mistake to think of "connected society" as a term of current political debate, to be deployed for tactical purposes against the language of the "Third Way", "progressive universalism" and other such mumbo-jumbo. Rather, in order to move the present discussion forward, we need to keep "connected society" to its given meaning: a society understood in terms of affection or personal tie.

As such, the idea embodies three insights. The first is that man is a social animal. People are not merely sterile economic agents, but living, breathing beings who find self-expression and identity in relation to each other. The second is that, in so doing, people create institutions, of an extraordinary range and diversity, and that these institutions themselves help to shape both the people who belong to them and society more widely. The third is that some of these institutions themselves stand between the individual and the state, acting among other things as buffers, conduits, outlets, and guarantors of stability.

This may seem pretty obvious—but the task of an explanation is often to rediscover or restate in other terms what we already know. Furthermore, this line of thought has quite radical policy implications, as we shall see. But these policies will be built on sand if we cannot spell out in a fairly punctilious way what a "connected society" amounts to and why it is valuable.

Start, then, with the basic idea of a society. At root, this derives from Roman law. In a society, the individuals are associates, or *socii* in Latin, who collectively belong and recognise each other as belonging, a recognition that creates a degree of mutual respect and obligation between them. These associates are equal and free, and the bond each owes to another derives its value from being freely given.

A society is thus in this basic sense an association free of class, hierarchy or any other inherited structure or institution that might constrain the freedom of individuals. And for the same reason, a society is and must be free from overwhelming concentrations of power. Power must be diffused; it must be shared and counterbalanced for a society to exist at all. The rule of law is both a prerequisite to and the specific creation of such power-sharing: institutions such as private property, or habeas corpus, or the independence of the judiciary naturally arise to protect existing freedoms and interests, and to permit new ones to develop. These institutions then serve as protectors of freedom in their turn.

A "connected society" goes one step further than this, however. It does not merely recognise the importance of institutions in the narrower, legal sense, such as those mentioned above: constitutional institutions whose role is to promote good order, restrain excessive power, and protect the basic freedoms of the citizen. It also recognises how institutions, conceived far more broadly, give shape and meaning to human lives. It takes the idea of mutual recognition that is implicit in the idea of society, and sees in it the aspect of personal regard, personal tie and personal affection that was missing, or perhaps assumed, in Hobbes and Oakeshott.

Edmund Burke is sometimes taken to be the father of this thought, in saying that "to be attached to the subdivision, to love the little platoon we belong to in society, is... the first link in the series by which we proceed towards a love to our country, and to mankind." It is a deeply small-c conservative idea. But it is not restricted to any political party or grouping. In Britain, it has strong resonances on the non-Fabian left, as we will see below. In the US, there is some overlap with traditions of community organisation and empowerment associated with the Chicago activist Saul Alinsky, who grafted onto them a radical politics of mass power and protest.

Burke, by contrast, is thinking of links in a web of institutions. We should not restrict ourselves to the little platoons, however; the regiment and the brigade are no less important, so to speak. And we should not even at this stage exclude institutions that have no physical presence at all. So we are talking not merely about a particular local church, or rugby club or branch of the Women's Institute; but also about the market, the nation state and the city; and, more abstractly still, about the family, marriage, and the rule of law.

These institutions are not created and sustained merely by physical or emotional affection, of course. They each have a point and purpose of their own. But even at their most distant and discreet, they retain some tie to us, some claim on our personal loyalty. That tie may be deep or shallow, long- or short-lived, near or far; it may be the surge of patriotism even the mildest of us feels when someone insults our country; it may be our automatic respect for a local doctor or vicar whom we have never even met; or it may be the joy of discovering in a remote Indian village that there is someone with a radio tuned into the Test match.

Yet equally, the idea of a "connected society" acknowledges that our feelings and affections are always somewhere present. It is they that underwrite our loyalty and investment in these institutions. And as Aristotle identified, and as the Romans first made into a principle of statecraft, the most natural, the most particular and the most universal of these feelings are those of friendship.

We are a long way from politics now. But already we can see in outline a restated critique of the growth of the state. Fabianism as a philosophy of state growth is a rationalist dogma; and state growth pushes us further towards an enterprise society. We already have noted its often pernicious social and economic effects. Oakeshott now helps us to see how it breeds authoritarianism, and abridges the rule of law.

But in fact the very possibility of society rests not on the concentration but on the diffusion of power. In a "connected society", the sovereign state is one institution, albeit a privileged one, among many. As citizens, we may owe it our moral allegiance, as Hobbes believed; but as associates we also owe allegiance to each other and to the many different institutions that define us. The state is uniquely endowed with the power to coerce individuals according to law against their will. But precisely for this reason, it is under continuing obligations. First, to be restrained in its own actions, recognising its intrinsic limitations, and balancing its own remedies with respect for existing arrangements and organisations; and secondly, to enfranchise and support those very institutions in our constitution that inhibit its power and force it into dialogue. One of the primary duties of our political leaders is to make and obey these self-denying ordinances—they are part of what it is to govern.

The Centrality of Institutions

We can see our institutions, then, as the crucial missing third part of the story so far. Instead of the opposition of the individual and the state to be found in traditional political theory, we have a three-way relation, between individuals, institutions and the state. It is this missing aspect of connection that transforms a society from a centralised, we-they, economic pushmi-pullyu into a living, flourishing organism.

But institutions are not just the objects of our loyalty and affection, and the relationships that help define us. They are also, in Burke's further thought, the repositories of much human wisdom and knowledge. Unless newly created, in order to exist at all they have fought their way against competitors, learnt from setbacks and profited from advantage. In short they have been formed by experience. They thus embody the collective experience of previous generations, and this experience can and frequently does outstrip the wisdom of those who would reform them. A conservative, it has been said, is someone who recognises that institutions are wiser than individuals. But from the present viewpoint it is not clear that this is a distinct political stance at all. On the contrary, it is simply irrational to ignore the wisdom of institutions. The political question is what weight, under given circumstances, this should bear in the creation of policy.

This is true even for institutions that have no physical presence at all. A financial market, for example, may simply appear as a collection of names and numbers on computer screens. Yet, as Adam Smith recognised, a market is not a memoryless place where pure economic agents come to transact. It is a cultural entity, situated within a rich context of human practices, traditions and expectations as to such things as pricing, weights and measures, quality of goods or services, delivery, returns and future behaviour. And it is governed by conventions and rules no less powerful for being inexplicit. Markets too, then, possess their own wisdom, disaggregated though they may be.

Of course, this is not to say that all tradition is good; that what exists must exist; or that our institutions never require further justification. But it reminds us that change is not reform, and that reform must go with the grain of institutions if it is to have a positive effect.

The history of British government is littered with attempts at reform that have ignored existing institutions and so undermined them; and, correspondingly, with late rediscoveries of the wisdom of some forgotten tradition. Take the case of friendly societies. Between 1800 and the beginning of the Second World War, there was a huge advance in voluntary provision for sickness and old age by means of these working class mutual-aid societies. By 1938 over 20 million working people were registered members. Even an early 19th century friendly society might provide benefits for sickness, unemployment and disability, as well as loans and a widow's pension. More services, including pensions, were added over time. It was run by the members and for the members on a one-member one-vote basis, so that costs were low and dishonest claims kept to a minimum. It was sustained by, and contributed to, a spirit of self-reliance and mutual support, which discouraged reliance on charity and on state provision.

The state first regulated friendly societies in an Act of 1793. Over the following century, legislation further defined the rights and responsibilities of those involved. It was only with the National Insurance Act of 1911, however, that the state inserted itself into the collection of contributions. It compelled all wage-earners between 16 and 70 to join a health benefit scheme, to which the state and employers also contributed. The scheme was, however, still administered by "approved" friendly societies and members were encouraged to make top-up contributions in their own right. When cuts in public expenditure were required, however, in 1922, 1925 and 1933, the Government did not hesitate to reduce the state subsidy to friendly societies, many of which ran into difficulties during the recession of the 1930s. They were ultimately relegated to the margins altogether when the administration of these benefits was nationalised in a series of acts after 1945. There was little reason for them to be effectively eliminated through crowding-out by the state, however, and similar voluntary institutions did not suffer this fate in much of Europe.

Fast forward to today, however, and what do we see? The UK's company pension schemes, which were once the envy of Europe, now have total deficits estimated at over £200 billion. They have been undermined by the unexpected withdrawal of tax relief in 1997 by Gordon Brown; but also by an earlier decision under the Thatcher government to tax the "overfunding" of schemes by their parent companies, which would have provided some buffer against present-day problems. Thus the wheel turns.

Connection and Identity

So far we have argued that human beings live in and through institutions. These institutions can be the objects of our loyalty and affection, they can mediate our relations with each other, and they can be the repositories of our inherited experience. We now need to look at how they interact with each other, how they can come together, and what effects this may have on our collective identity.

When we examine a particular society under the headings of civility or enterprise, we can see the state as sovereign authority in traditional categories, whether as passive enabler or as active, ambitious agent. In a connected society, however, the emphasis is not on the state at all but on culture and identity, on how people think of themselves, and why. This line of thought applies to all human societies, in principle; all may be seen in terms of connection, just as they can be seen in terms of civility or enterprise. But to see its political relevance today, we need to focus on British society, and on the well-springs of our own identity: on such things as our language and literature, our school history, our contribution to the rule of law, our experience of empire and its aftermath, and our traditions of teamwork, decency, irony, dissent and wit.

In so doing, we can think of the thread of cultural exchange once more in the spirit of Oakeshott: as that of a conversation or dialogue. Different institutions, from different traditions, each have their own distinctive "voices": those of science, business, religion, the law, education, or the arts, for example. In a conversation each voice has its own character, yet each must speak in common terms to others if it is to be understood, to move, to persuade, or to command. How they develop, how they interact with each other, and how they are heard by different people, will determine the character of the conversation as a whole. Similarly, the character of a society will derive from the way in which its own cultural conversation develops, and is encouraged to develop.

The conversational metaphor is a rich one. In the first place, any conversation demands a context of mutual respect and order, in short, of civility. This is a basic rule of conduct between citizens dealing with each other under the rule of law. In any conversation all voices have their place, and though they may be ignored once speaking, none is to be forbidden in advance from speaking at all. All are, in effect, regarded as autonomous and individual. Moreover, a vibrant conversation is one whose voices are diverse, mature, self-confident and independent: in short the voices of citizens, able to examine authority, to question it, and to hold it to account. And finally, conversation reminds us of the different possible roles of the media: as a purveyor of ideas that in principle aspires to be neutral between them; as a critic or advocate of established power; and as a voice advocating its own ideas or interests in the attempt to wield power for itself. As the internet and new communications technologies continue to expand the range of conversation, our sensitivity to these different roles can only increase.

It is a distinctively European achievement to have first developed and brought together the fundamental institutions—the nation state, the rights of individuals as citizens to speak and associate freely, the marketplace, the political forum—through which our cultural conversation takes place, and from which it continues to spread out into the world. And it is this insistence on the acknowledgement of civil authority expressed through the rule of law that specifically differentiates the European tradition from, for example, classical Islamic traditions, in which law and religion do not merely run alongside and reinforce one other, but are regarded as identical.

The idea of conversation also brings out what is most distinctive in the constitutional settlement in the USA. The genius of the American founders, and above all of James Madison, was to engineer a constitution that deliberately constrained and fragmented the power of government between state and federal levels; between executive, legislature and judiciary; and between House of Representatives and Senate. Each was thereby placed as a check and balance to another;

and so all were forced into continuing conversation with each other, as to the issues of the day, and as to the proper scope and limits of the various parts of government itself.

Finally, the metaphor of conversation underlines the wider critique offered here. The last government was characterised by a default instinct to extend the powers of the state over the lives of its citizens. In conversational terms, one might think of the state as the domineering bore at the table, whose loudness overwhelms the talk of others. But a better parallel might be that of the patriarch whose favourites thrive, but in whose unspeaking presence others feel robbed of air and automatically fall silent. Similarly, the extension of the state, whatever its apparent short-term attractions, tends to undermine the voices, the energy and the creativity of its citizens. If it is hard to see this now, that may partly be because we have lost sight of how rich and fulfilled all human life has the potential to be.

The Strength of Diversity

The present emphasis on diversity and conversation does not merely spring from the conviction that these are valuable in their own right or as a means of social enrichment. We can think of them as crucial sources of social intelligence.

There is now a huge literature on the theory of "wise crowds": the phenomenon whereby diverse groups make better judgements, or solve problems better than experts. To be "wise", a group must satisfy four conditions: its members must be diverse, independent (each person exercising his or her own view, and not deferring to others), and decentralised (so people can specialise or draw on local knowledge).

Finally, there must be some means to aggregate or gather their private judgements or choices together into a collective decision.

When these conditions are met, the results can be astounding. Compared to experts, crowds are generally better at estimating things (such as the weight of a rendered and dressed ox, in a 1906 experiment of Francis Galton); quicker at accurately assessing outcomes (such as the reason why the Challenger space shuttle blew up); better at predicting the results of sporting events; and better at picking stocks and shares. And interestingly, it turns out that groups consisting of experts are regularly less good than groups that also include non-experts under testable laboratory conditions.

It is perhaps no accident that the idea of a "connected society" that we have identified emphasises precisely the things that make crowds wise. Its whole focus is on promoting diversity, independent-mindedness and decentralisation, and much of the point of its insistence on markets and conversation is to enable these important aggregators of human opinion to function effectively. By the same token, however, other viewpoints seem to destroy social wisdom. Paternalism of any stamp encourages deference to officials and experts, and "groupthink", or the herd instinct. The present statism is worse still. It undermines diversity, reduces independence and increases centralisation. A better recipe for foolishness in a society would be hard to imagine.

More generally, the theory of wise crowds adds force to our critique of enterprise society, or one organised from above as a single purposive entity. It suggests that such societies have an inherent tendency to lack wisdom and hence social and economic success, compared to more diverse and pluralistic models. The paradox here is that the attempt to organise society as an enterprise in fact kills enterprise. On the contrary, it is only insofar as societies are genuinely empowering of individual energy and creativity that they can succeed.

Nevertheless, there is an obvious objection to this line of thought. Now this talk of conversation is all very well, it runs. But it's really just soft-centred jaw-jaw, isn't it? Just donnish after-dinner pass-the-port self-indulgence, the kind of worthy but irrelevant theorising we have come to expect from those who lack the power to take tough decisions in the real world. In the real world, not everyone is civilised. There's not much point meeting bombs, crime and hatred with fine words.

In fact, however, this argument is a weak one. There is little reason why a nation committed to the values of a connected society should be anything less than utterly resolute in defending them. Quite the contrary: the history of warfare suggests that it is often those very values that have inspired the greatest achievements on the battlefield. The Athenian statesman Pericles made this point in his funeral oration of 431 BC, in contrasting the openness and democratic values of Athens with the narrow military authoritarianism of its bitter rival, Sparta:

> *Our system of government does not copy the institutions of our neighbours. It is more the case of our being a model to others... Our constitution is called a democracy because power is in the hands not of a minority but of the whole people... There is a great difference between us and our opponents in our attitude towards military security... [and] certain advantages, I think, in our way of meeting danger voluntarily, with an easy mind, instead of with a laborious training, with natural rather than with state-induced courage.*

Similarly, in combatting terrorism, the first battlefield is over the hearts and minds of a nation's own citizens and residents. Of those who fret that a concern for free institutions and cultural conversation mean weakness we can simply ask: what are you seeking to defend?

The British Experience

We have now described the idea of a "connected society" more fully. Our claim is that it is this conception of society that lies behind the politicians' Big Society; and this that should be the central focus of British policy-making. Indeed there is a challenge here for all of us: to recognise, protect and enhance our connected society, and seek to enrich the cultural conversation within it.

The idea of a "connected society" implies certain limitations. It discourages the concentration of power in any particular organisation or person, public or private. It is self-aware and modest in its expectations for government. It understands the need for economic growth, but it does not regard economic growth as the only source of well-being. It does not favour any particular section or group within society, except for supporting those in poverty, who may lack the capability to play a proper part in society at all, whether that lack is of cash, experience or opportunity.

However, the idea of a "connected society" is far from modest in its optimism and ambitions, for individuals themselves and for the multifarious ways in which they grow and develop. It recognises the social bond that we each owe to one another, and the role of institutions in creating and strengthening that bond. Here again, the idea of conversation can guide us to the right way forward: to trust people;

to invest in their virtues and not their faults; to welcome aspiration, energy, innovation and plurality; and to support and extend the institutions that carry on our distinct traditions as a nation.

But the counterpart of a connected or Big Society is a different conception of the individuals that make it up. We need to ask ourselves, in short, what a human being really is.

7 **The Danger of Happiness**

> If you're poor I hope you get rich
> If you're rich I hope you get happy
> *Bob Dylan*

Welcome to Theory X and Theory Y.

Theory X holds that people are natural shirkers, who will avoid work whenever possible. They are gullible and unambitious. They resist change, dislike responsibility and will only work if coerced or bribed towards an organisation's goals. Theory Y, by contrast, holds that people are naturally inclined to work, whether in their jobs or at play. They are naturally enterprising, and willing to use their own ingenuity to solve problems. But that ingenuity is rarely tested in large organisations.

Here's the rub: whatever the reality, belief in Theory X is self-fulfilling. If people are treated in a Theory X way, they become demoralised and unproductive. Those in charge then assume that this is how people really are—entrenching Theory X in their minds—and become still more controlling. This leads to more demoralisation, and so on. Controlling people thus worsens performance and service, generating more failure and more control.

As people rise through Theory X organisations, they become increasingly selected for, and wedded to, a Theory X view of the world.

Seeing others as merely financially motivated, they come to see themselves and their organisations as so. Altruism comes to seem costly and irrelevant to the real action, philanthropy merely a matter of public display. They take the modern emphasis on profit maximisation as a licence, indeed a requirement, to trade in any area that generates net income. The task of creating and perfecting some product or service becomes secondary. Indeed the very idea of perfecting a product, with its implication of open-ended cost, becomes a source of suspicion.

Something similar has happened in this country in recent years. Urged on by a government which was preoccupied with personal wealth and financial success, our great institutions of state have moved towards a Theory X view of people, both their employees and clients. The result has been demoralisation and inefficiency. Part of the Big Society project is to return us to Theory Y.

In particular, over the past 40 years the public understanding of human behaviour has increasingly reflected a standard view of man as perfectly rational, greedy and fearful, and hyper-sensitive to marginal gains and losses. This standard economic view has become a default position, as we have seen. But as Theory X reminds us, it has also been propagated by many large organisations, including corporations and government itself.

But this economic view has not had it all its own way. On the contrary, there has also been a huge and growing literature of reaction. The counter-cultural views of the 1960s—that there is more to life than money, that economics can never do justice to the complexity and richness of human life and human experience, and that we should live for the day—are increasingly mainstream. They feed into claims, charted in books such as *Affluenza* and *The Spirit Level*, that materialism is creating an epidemic of depression and social breakdown as people find themselves aspiring to what they cannot achieve and unable to compete with their peers. It has been supplemented by growing fears about the impact of globalisation and turbulence in the global market economy. The result is conflict: we reject conventional economic thinking, but without quite knowing why. We yearn for an alternative, but we have nothing coherent to offer.

One result of this conflict has been the rise of "happiness theory", promoted in such recent bestsellers as *Happiness: Lessons from a New Science* by Richard Layard, a noted economist and former professor at the London School of Economics. Happiness theory is not simply the ancient idea that what really matters is happiness rather than, say, wealth or income. Rather, it claims that people's happiness can be measured; that happiness can be compared, managed and traded off as between different groups of people; that policy ideas should be assessed on the basis of its contribution to happiness; and indeed that the overall goal of public policy should be to maximise happiness.

At first glance it may look as though this emphasis on happiness is a counterblast to neoclassical economics. After all, economic growth is not the be-all and end-all of human existence. And isn't the whole point of happiness theory to reject the caricature image of man as *Homo Economicus*?

In fact, however, happiness theory subtly reinforces the conventional picture: by simply substituting one set of human motivations for another, it leaves intact the broader framework of perfect information, perfect rationality and marginal preferences that is so deeply problematic. Indeed it legitimates that framework. With their obvious worries about human psychology addressed, it becomes yet harder for those that disagree to articulate their deeper concerns.

Many people have argued against Layard's "happiness theory", for different reasons. The real point, however, is that in one key respect it is fundamentally and dangerously misconceived. At its heart is exactly the kind of passive conception of the human self that we find in neoclassical economics itself.

But the story is not entirely bleak. For in contrast to this passive idea we can develop a positive, active and dynamic conception of the self, rooted in an ancient but ignored philosophical tradition dating back to Plato and the Ancient Greeks. This active self gives us a route from Theory X to Theory Y. Once we have this in hand, we can return much more fruitfully to our earlier questions about the status and nature of economics, and its role in public policy.

Layard and *Happiness*

To get to grips properly with the issues we really need a clear target to aim at, and the best place to start is with Professor Layard's book *Happiness*. Layard deserves great credit for focusing public attention on the issue, and on some of the causes, of unhappiness. His book has been both influential and controversial, and we cannot hope to do justice to it here. Nevertheless, a key part of the argument can be briefly summarised.

Layard is a follower of the English philosopher Jeremy Bentham, founder of utilitarianism, and with Bentham he believes that happiness is "hedonic" or based on pleasure: it is a state of mind, and the goal of public policy is to maximise the pleasure experienced through this state of mind by the largest possible number of people.

Particular attention has focused on two claims. The first, reflecting a standard economic view of consumption, says that after a certain point greater wealth contributes diminishing marginal amounts of happiness. An extra £1,000 does not make the billionaire any happier, for example, but is usually a huge source of happiness to someone on the minimum wage. The second claim is that a person's happiness is a relative or positional matter: that it largely depends on changes in their status or position relative to their peers. On this view, it is of no relevance to Mr Smith's happiness how he fares compared to the Duke of Westminster. What matters to him is keeping up with the Joneses. Not only that: the desire for status forces people into a rat race. They work harder, but one person's relative gain is another's relative loss, so there is no net social benefit at all.

For Layard, these views have two specific implications: one for taxation, one for public spending. The first is to create a moral case for high levels of taxation. In his view greater equality of income generates greater net happiness, because redistributing wealth confers happiness on the recipient at little cost to the (relatively well-off) person paying out. Moreover, he thinks higher taxes also counteract the rat race, by discouraging people from working harder. They thus contribute to a better work-life balance.

The second effect is to allow him to argue for huge public expenditure on addressing mental illness by such means as cognitive psychotherapy and the wide-scale provision of psychotherapeutic drugs. These treatments may be expensive. But the cost is, he estimates, vastly less than the happiness gains that relief from depression brings.

Layard's views have been much debated. Some commentators have questioned their factual basis, claiming that they are dependent on data which have been mispresented, and undersupported by evidence. Others have argued that that they are internally inconsistent and methodologically flawed. Yet others have claimed that they are paternalistic, undemocratic and inhumane in their conclusions.

But the deepest problem is none of these. It is that the whole argument is really a blind alley. It has been a truism since the time of Aristotle that the term "happiness" can cover many things. There is no single and stable concept in common use. Rather, the term has been used over the years in connection with a bewildering range of different ideas including well-being, self-fulfilment, blessedness, virtue, excellence, skill, moral or physical health, the full possession of one's faculties, wealth or property, honour, virtue and cultivated tastes, to name only a few.

But what about pleasure? Following Bentham, Layard identifies happiness with pleasure, and this allows him to use what people report about their feelings of pleasure as evidence for his theory. However, in so doing he crucially assumes, as we have seen, that happiness is fundamentally a state of mind. But if this is true, if happiness is just a matter of how we feel, then it is easy to improve our national happiness immediately. All that is necessary is to put Prozac or some other mind-pleasing drug into our water-supplies. Of course to do so would be absurd: among other things it would be an outrageous infringement of personal liberty. Yet in his advocacy of government provision of psychotherapeutic drugs on a mass basis, Layard comes close to this very view. On his account, the opium of the people is opium.

What has gone wrong here? The key point is that nothing in the underlying theory has really changed. Layard purports to reshape policy around a new and missing category and thereby to make it more reflective of and more relevant to actual human needs. In reality, however, what he has done is to take one unclear and unspecifiable value, "utility", replace it with another, "happiness", and then draw dubious policy conclusions on that basis. The remainder of the standard picture remains, with all its hidden problems and flawed presuppositions intact. Indeed, as noted, it is tacitly reinforced and further enfranchised by the appearance of change, and by the new rhetoric of happiness.

After all, it is not as though happiness has been missing from economic thought over the past two centuries. On the contrary, some notion of happiness or other has been assumed by economic debate from the beginning. A key point of the theory of GDP over the years, for example, has been to develop a broadly well-understood and quantifiable proxy for national happiness, well-being or benefit. It may or may not have succeeded—opinions vary on this question. But the world's macroeconomists are hardly smacking their heads post-Layard from a sudden realisation that their subject is really about happiness. For almost all of them, it has been about happiness all along.

The Passive Self

Thus the real significance of happiness theory lies in what it leaves untouched: a deeply passive conception of what a human being is. We noted earlier that in standard economics people are not flesh-and-blood human beings but "agents" whose behaviour can be mathematically specified and modelled. In fact, however, even this language overstates the case: within the theory they are not even in any interesting sense agents, or indeed individuals, at all. Instead they are vessels for "utility", or bearers of preferences. Layard's happiness theory perpetuates this view. Happiness is merely a state of mind, and people are passive recipients of happiness. They are empty dials, which only flicker into life when some temporary pleasure pulses through them.

This view of the self as passive is not merely embedded in our standard economics. On the contrary, it permeates our intellectual history, most notably in some empiricist traditions that see humans as mere recipients of sensory inputs or external impressions. (Yet it is interesting to note that the idea of man as purely self-interested was given an early and trenchant refutation by David Hume, close friend of Adam Smith and arguably the greatest empiricist philosopher of them all, in his *Enquiry Concerning the Principles of Morals*.)

And the idea of people as passive selves is also deeply rooted in contemporary British life. It lies behind what many see as an administrative culture which has become increasingly dumbed-down and risk-averse, which sets our children low educational and moral standards, which undervalues achievement, and which too readily accepts the second-rate. That culture draws on a pap idea of marketing as feeding the lowest urges of the widest segment of the population. It is neurotically afraid of abstract ideas and diverse achievement. It caters for people, rather than challenging them.

So this assumption that people are fundamentally passive has disastrous effects. But what is the alternative? Is there—to put the matter at its most abstract—an alternative conception of the self, of what it is to be human, which can be used to guide public policy? And if so, what difference would it make to our politics, to our public culture, to our national identity?

To answer this question we need to pull together various ideas that at first glance may seem only distantly related to each other. We begin in the 4th century BC, with Plato's dialogue *The Republic*. *The Republic* is often seen, not without reason, as a rather authoritarian work. But early on Plato uses an imagined conversation about the nature of justice between Socrates and his followers to develop a profoundly worthwhile idea. Socrates thinks that the just person is happier than the unjust one, and in arguing for this he talks about happiness as a kind of self-fulfilment, and in particular as a matter of what he calls "doing your own thing". His thought seems to be that everyone has a distinctive capability or function, and happiness is a matter of developing that capability to the utmost.

We can find something similar in Aristotle. In the *Nicomachean Ethics*, Aristotle focuses on the role of action and habit in engendering happiness. Man is a social animal, he believes: humans are innately gregarious beings, who are embedded in social relationships. Happiness is always the end-goal and result of action, he suggests; and indeed it is itself a kind of activity, one of living well. Again, there is a connection to virtue: the person who repeatedly acts well becomes virtuous, in Aristotle's view, as good actions settle over time into good habits.

We can catch a glimpse of a similar line of thought even in Locke, writing two millennia later from what is in many ways the radically different perspective of a Christian philosopher in his *Second Treatise of Government*. For Locke humans are naturally free and autonomous beings, who have been given the Earth in common. But in that case, if the Earth is their common inheritance, how can they come to own private property at all?

Locke's answer is that they own their own labour, and it is what he calls the "mixing" of this labour with other objects that confers a right of ownership to those objects, and so gives rise to the institution of private property. Thus the farmer who cultivates open land thereby establishes rights of ownership over that land—but, it should be noted, only so much as he can directly cultivate. Hence this process of mixing labour has a natural end, and property rights have an intrinsically human scale.

Scholars have toiled long and hard to attack Locke's idea of "mixing one's labour" as unclear or obviously mistaken. What does it mean? Is labour the kind of thing that can be mixed with an object at all? What happens when all the "open land" is occupied? Isn't Locke's idea simply a charter for self-enrichment by the haves over the have-nots?

However, if we read the idea of mixing one's labour less literally and take it as a metaphor, it starts to look not merely not wrong, but importantly right. In effect, Locke is suggesting humans have a natural drive to shape, and so to personalise, their environments. Not only that, but these actions can in turn ground even the most fundamental institutions, such as rights to property.

Capabilities and the Active Self

The idea of a human being as fundamentally a bundle of capabilities, or of humans as striving for self-expression through the exercise of those capabilities, is not restricted to one philosophical or political tradition, however. On the contrary, it is astonishingly widespread. We can find it throughout the Christian tradition, of course, for example in St Paul's Epistle to the Romans. But it also features prominently in Hinduism, in the idea of Atma-Jnana or self-realisation; in the writings of the existentialists; in the work of the American psychologist Abraham Maslow; and prominently in the *1844 Manuscripts* of Karl Marx. It is an idea which rises above racial, political or religious categories.

With this in mind, we can assemble the broad outline of a completely different conception of the human self, and so of human well-being, to the passive one described above. It has three distinct components, which link the ideas of action, self-fulfilment, and social institutions.

In this view the human self is not static but a dynamic, active force. It is autonomous, imaginative and creative, and its needs and interests constantly change and develop over time. It has actual and potential capabilities that naturally seek an outlet for self-expression. Moreover, people are social beings. They are not merely gregarious; rather, they have an instinct to change and personalise what is around them, and to link with others. Over time human actions create habits, and good habits become virtues; shared habits over time create practices; and practices that have developed over time become institutions.

Now at this point the reader may be rather sceptical about the key idea of "doing your own thing", with its overtones of Timothy Leary, Sergeant Pepper and the Summer of Love. Isn't the problem precisely that everyone nowadays is always doing their own thing? Instead, don't we need more discipline, more deference to authority and a return to traditional values?

But in fact this is not a call for a more permissive society; or for more narcissism in government, something of which the UK is rarely in short supply. Properly understood, "doing your own thing" both frees and constrains our understanding of human self-fulfilment.

First of all, it invites people to ask themselves what they stand for; what they care about, what they want to become, and what they can achieve. In short, who they are. Secondly, it is both highly personalised and optimistic about human potential. How you do your own thing may well radically differ from how I do mine. Everyone has, or can develop, his or her own distinctive skills or goals or capabilities. Personal success becomes a matter of fulfilling one's potential, not simply of a status rat race against others. Thirdly, it is egalitarian and non-hierarchical: we each have our own capabilities, so you and I can always learn from each other. But we are equals. Because humans have such astonishing potential in so many different directions, there is no single metric—least of all IQ—on which different people can be comprehensively assessed.

This line of thought is massively incomplete, of course—in particular, nothing has been said as to whether or how different capabilities should or even could be valued for policy purposes. But it is not presumptuous to suggest that it offers the kernel of a far richer and more dynamic basis for public policy than the dismal assumptions presently on offer. This is brought out by its affinity with a well worked-out theory of capabilities developed over the past 20 years by the welfare economist and philosopher Amartya Sen.

Beginning in 1979, Sen has argued that public policy should seek to benefit not such things as a person's utility, or access to basic goods, or equality of outcome or opportunity, but rather their capabilities. For Sen, these capabilities are very wide-ranging. They include basic bodily functions such as resistance to disease, situational advantages such as access to good nourishment, as well as more advanced capabilities such as the ability to earn a living, or to manage one's life independently, or to realise one's talents.

This is a very attractive approach. It is not excessively materialist. It is positive, indeed idealistic, about people. It is open-ended and pluralist in its idea of the good life and of human flourishing. It stresses the institutions, habits, practices and culture from which capabilities spring and to which they contribute. It recognises that human happiness is too varied to be precisely defined, but is a by-product of action, and especially of the drive to self-fulfilment. And it brings out, crucially, a two-way relationship between freedom and capability. Capabilities require a certain freedom to be exercised. But people must have an adequate range of basic capabilities in the first place if they are to exercise their freedoms at all. Inspired by Sen, therefore, a theory of capabilities can dovetail very well with our earlier discussion of the connected society: it can both ground support for public services, with a special focus on those at the margins of society; and generate a richer conception of what a society as a whole can achieve.

But the present emphasis is rather different. Sen is fundamentally arguing with an eye to developing countries, and his feels like an aggregative, top-down approach to policy-making. The present perspective is far more individual and bottom-up. For us, the challenge is not merely to change how government sees us, the people. It is to change how we see ourselves.

Rethinking Incentives

It should be clear by now that there is a radical difference between the view outlined here and the standard *rigor mortis* view of human beings to be found in textbook economics. In particular, the idea of the active self implies a quite different view of human motivation, with potentially revolutionary implications for private and public sector alike, as we shall see.

As it happens, there has been a huge amount of research work in recent years to understand the nature of human motivation. The picture is far from complete, but in broad terms it massively supports the capability view. Indeed, it suggests that the carrot-and-stick approach of conventional economics is often not merely a misreading of what actually drives people, but actually counter-productive. When implemented, it does not improve people's performance. It actually serves to undermine it.

Thus external rewards can work well in encouraging people to work harder in routine tasks. But a huge amount of academic literature suggests that in creative tasks, they are typically counter-productive. Highly incentivised people do worse, not better, than those who are working on a steady salary (or nothing) and doing a job for the sake of it. Children who are given contingent (if-you-do-this-then-you-get-this) rewards for tasks they enjoy tend to lose, not gain, interest in those tasks. Arts students who report higher intrinsic motivation are more professionally successful 20 years later. Scientists who are given a measure of autonomy and not penalised for early failure generate more, and higher-quality, research than do those who are heavily reviewed and rewarded (or not) on results. Free and open source software programmers respond most to intrinsic, not external, motivations. Civil servants who are incentivised by performance-related pay are less effective than those who are paid in the normal way.

The effect of high rewards or similar in creative jobs is thus very often to encourage people to misallocate their effort between tasks, to fixate on a given target, to take too much or too little risk, to have foreshortened time horizons, to behave unethically in order to get what they want, and to experience debilitating levels of stress and anxiety. In short: rather an accurate description of the culture of many parts of the current financial markets.

Psychologists following Abraham Maslow have long distinguished between three different accounts of what drives human behaviour. One is biological: the primeval need to eat, drink and procreate—what Daniel Pink has called Motivation 1.0. The second drive is (*rigor-mortis*) economic: the idea that people are purely motivated by external incentives of gain and loss—Motivation 2.0. The third drive is based on human capabilities and intrinsic rewards—Motivation 3.0.

The effect of recent research is to make clear yet again the limitations of a purely economic Motivation 2.0-style account of human beings, and to push us towards a capability approach.

So what, then, is Motivation 3.0? It is based on three ideas: autonomy, mastery and purpose. "Autonomy" refers to the degree of control people feel they have over their work; "mastery" to their desire to get better at something they care about; and "purpose" to their desire for meaning—for what they are doing to matter not merely to them but to others, or to God. People succeed—both in the world's terms and their own—when they are motivated by intrinsic rewards, not external ones. Their success is most influenced not by talent but by sheer hard work and persistence, in seeking a mastery that can never be fully realised. And the work or sport or pursuit in question is driven by the belief that, in a world of hype, it matters. Ultimately, then, conviction and substance are what make the difference.

The Science of Compassion

Together, these ideas of autonomy, mastery and purpose provide huge empirical support for what we have called the active self. For the active self, the self as a bundle of capabilities, is naturally engaged with its environment and with others around it. If the passive self is, metaphorically, an atom cut off from others, then the active self has carbon bonds constantly seeking to link with others. It is other-regarding.

But the deeper point is that only an active conception of the self allows for the possibility of compassion. Only an active self can act in a way that expresses fellow-feeling. The active self is thus the common prerequisite to both compassionate conservatism and the connected or Big society. On this view people are naturally compassionate; their self-fulfilment involves the development and exercise of their capabilities; and the expression of these capabilities in action is something for which they can be held properly responsible.

These claims may seem wild. But in fact there is an increasing amount of scientific evidence for them. In particular, recent research by Jean Decety and others suggests that there is a neural basis for compassion or empathy in the human brain. Thus people who observe others in pain, especially their partners, seem to process this recognition in part through their own pain centres. People who consider the emotional reactions of others process this through their own emotional neural systems. By contrast, certain autistic, narcissistic and anti-social personality disorders manifest themselves in a lack of empathy, or may cause their victims to not even recognise others as people at all.

Overall, then, there is good reason to think that people are naturally compassionate. Moreover, compassion gives purpose to our lives, and as such is deeply psychologically rewarding. Thus several studies suggest that people who regularly give money, time or support to others enjoy better physical and mental health, have lower levels of depression and suicide and have increased longevity, compared to those who do not. Those who donate to charity report higher levels of happiness than others. People who volunteer have lower mortality rates, greater bodily functioning and lower rates of depression later in life than those who do not volunteer, especially if they spend more than 100 hours per year in volunteering, and if it involves repeated personal contact in helping strangers.

But the exercise of compassion is ultimately one of the most basic resources of society itself. To continue our earlier metaphor: if the active self is an atom with carbon bonds, then families are small molecules, other institutions are larger ones, and society itself is the largest molecule of all. It has no fixed shape—it can be of any shape depending on how its individuals and institutions link together. But on its shape and composition depend many if not all of its characteristics. Society is not prior to human individuality, as Aristotle would have it; the two are co-dependent.

This allows us to resolve an apparent paradox. As *The Spirit Level* underlines, different societies can and do have different characteristics. They can have massively different levels of social capital. But this does not mean we have to think of a society as something over and above its component individuals and institutions, and potentially with interests opposed to theirs. Different societies can be more or less successful, and the role and efficacy of the state can be an important part of the difference. But far more important are the energy and effectiveness of those individuals and institutions. How to improve that energy and effectiveness is arguably the central public policy challenge of the present day—and the challenge taken up by the Big Society.

The Threat to Altruism?

But the fact that compassion is a natural human instinct does not mean it is safe from threat. On the contrary, the instinct for compassion must be nurtured.

Recent neurological research suggests that the instinct to engage and co-operate with others is mainly developed in the early teen years.

Not only that, but our willingness to treat others fairly and in a trusting way is heavily affected by the environment in which we grow up: "high trust" environments encourage "high trust" behaviour, and "low trust" environments encourage "low trust" behaviour. Early-life experiences create chemical pathways in the brain that reinforce feelings of fair dealing with others, and set expectations of such fair dealing in return — or not.

Yet many young people in Britain today grow up in conditions of great stress. They live in small and crowded city housing stock, and very often flats. They have limited access to green space and to regular exercise, while TV and computer games dominate their free time. On average, they spend only half an hour a day in "purposeful outdoor activity". The result is that more than one in five young people suffers from mental health problems, while rates of suicide and self-harm among the young continue to rise.

The growing possibility is that for many young people today it may be psychologically difficult to experience feelings of altruism, and so of fraternity or compassion, at all. Lacking a strong sense of trust, they may find it hard to offer trust to others and so simply opt out, thus in turn reinforcing feelings of alienation and disaffection. What they need is to be treated as human beings, as valuable in themselves. Yet they are losing their connection with others, and with nature. They face a world from which the personal dimension, the human touch, has largely been removed.

The issue could hardly be more serious, concerning as it does the squandering of so much talent and potential, and thus the very possibility of whether many young people can have a worthwhile place within British society at all. Its implications in a world of increasing gun and knife crime are also obvious.

So What?

But so what? Fine words, you might say, but this brief foray into philosophical ideas is just an academic exercise. So maybe government hasn't got it quite right. But these are pettifogging distinctions, which no politician could be expected to consider or even remember. They really make no practical difference. Policy rolls on, after all.

You could not be more wrong. Moving to a capabilities approach, and to this dynamic conception of human possibility, completely changes how we should view policy, and indeed politics itself. The crucial point is that a deep belief in the capabilities of others is a prerequisite of greater trust in government, and in society as a whole. A politics of responsibility requires an active conception of the self. You cannot trust someone you despise, and our present system of government despises people—both the people who work in it and the people whom it is designed to serve. It uses the rhetoric of empowerment, but its view of people is so debased that the result is confusion and failure.

The first thing a capabilities approach changes is the role of government. At present, as we have seen, the machinery of British government is presently very top-down, centralised, micro-managerial and hostile to intelligent innovation. A capabilities agenda changes all this. Government becomes far more pluralist, and cautious about intervening in people's lives. It sets standards and rules, and enforces them—but then it trusts people to do their own thing. So it might, for example, make available funding in blocks rather than prescribing how it is to be spent. It might prefer grants of money to voluntary organisations, rather than contracts. And it would devolve power to independent institutions, and hold them periodically accountable for outcomes.

The move to capabilities also pushes public policy to be far more holistic. It can take decisions based on a rich conception of human good, and not only a pounds, shillings and pence justification. Freed from the requirement to regard people as merely economic agents, policymakers can look more at what is actually happening, and why. It becomes possible to explain why certain personal qualities matter whose value cannot be modelled economically: qualities like loyalty, energy, personal warmth and creativity. It becomes possible to see how certain social phenomena have a cultural and not merely an economic basis. It becomes possible to understand the causes and effects of social frustration as a cause of social failure, and the quest for social status as a result.

Take teenage pregnancy, for example. The conventional wisdom on the centre-right is that teenage pregnancy is an economic reaction to a benefits system that supports, and so encourages, very young mothers who have children by giving them increased benefits and priority access to social housing. In some cases this may well be true—but it is only a part of a wider explanation. As anyone who has worked with teenage mothers will tell you, these pregnancies are often a reaction to lack of love, lack of status, or lack of a role in life. A teenage girl is a young woman at a very vulnerable stage of her life. As a mother, she automatically takes on a role—and a role of some status, which demands the attention of others. Is it any wonder if, seeing this and perhaps without much experience or resources or family support, she ends up pregnant?

Not only that: a recent study shows that in the most deprived areas of the UK people have nearly two decades less of healthy life than those in the most affluent ones. The effect of this seems to be to encourage women from the poorest backgrounds to have children on average a decade earlier, at 20 rather than 30. Richer women have a strong incentive to delay childbirth while they invest in their education, development and careers, in the expectation that they will have much longer healthy lives.

The point is clear: many social phenomena cannot simply be understood through standard economic models. Social policy cannot simply be carried out through attempts to influence human behaviour through tweaking marginal incentives, via traditional instruments of authority such as better policing. It must range far more widely.

Finally, the move to a capabilities approach opens up and invigorates public debate. The very idea of a debate or conversation is based on respect, on each treating the other as a participant in a shared activity. The Blair government's attempt at a Big Conversation was fatuous because no-one genuinely believed it did or ever could have respect for those taking part. The present approach, by contrast, sees every person as a fizzing bundle of actual or potential capability. Its principle is that all are to be respected, all are equal at the table. It means a limit to deference—be that deference to people, to theory or simply to power as such—and the steady embracing of evidence, experience, common sense, practical skill and institutional wisdom across a variety of fields. It works with the grain of human beings, not against it. And it is for these reasons that a capabilities approach is profoundly conservative.

Secondary Schools: A Case Study

The capabilities approach is a viewpoint, which can structure how we look at all public policy. Let us close this chapter by looking at the difference it could make to our secondary schools.

This is an area in which policy has long insulted the abilities of teachers, staff and students alike. The national curriculum has expanded to fill the entire teaching time of most state schools. Under the Blair and Brown governments it effectively specified on a lesson-by-lesson basis across a whole range of subjects what the teacher was to teach, week on week, month on month over the year. There has been little flexibility or scope for initiative in the classroom, and an endless testing regime that distorted teaching priorities and pedestrianised the classroom experience. Performance targets for pupils have often displaced real learning.

Inadequate account has been taken of the difference between good and bad teachers—making it virtually impossible to remove a bad teacher from their position. Such was the preoccupation with academic outcomes that other activities have been relegated to the sidelines. Meanwhile school heads were endlessly bombarded with paperwork from the then Department of Children, Schools and Families and "guidance" from ancillary quangos setting out new central priorities and initiatives. Running through the whole system was an ideology of government in which education was seen as a matter of skills provision for industry, and schools regarded simply as buildings—although there is little real evidence that good buildings as such improve educational outcomes.

Little wonder, then, that many people in education are heavily preoccupied with levels of funding, as though funding differentials were all that separated good schools from bad. Little wonder that so many good school heads have succeeded only by bucking the system, or that so many teachers suffer from poor morale. Little wonder that achievement remains stubbornly low in so many schools.

Worst of all: little wonder that so many pupils, having spent so much time without much real learning at school, become disaffected with learning as such. A 2008 Ofsted report found that 45% of schools surveyed failed to give an adequate conceptual grasp of mathematics to pupils. The most recent OECD study found that British children start their education younger and have longer school days than most other developed countries. Yet among 29 countries, only Mexico, Turkey and Israel keep fewer children in school after the age of 16.

This dire state of affairs is the result of many hands. But it has been profoundly influenced by our standard model of economics and its associated pathologies of government. Every effort has been made to control people from the centre. Vital but intangible values such as those of teaching morale, pride and public service have been underplayed in favour of incentives designed to tweak behaviour. Trust has been driven out of the system.

A capabilities approach would change all this. It would see education not merely as skills training or as necessary to meet national manpower needs, but as a way into life in all its diversity: as a matter of learning to be human. This implies a different notion of what a school is: not a collection of buildings but an institution, and not standardised but each different in its own way. It implies a belief that a comprehensive education should not simply be about open access and needs-blind admission, but should be comprehensive in its sense of human possibility. It implies a drastic scaling-back of the national curriculum, and public encouragement for outside activities such as sports, art, drama, public speaking and above all music, which allow young people to stretch themselves in different directions. And it seeks to enable the creation of new schools—be they publicly or privately funded, and in corporate, trust or co-operative form.

The same sense of human possibility applies to its treatment of teachers and heads. It would drastically reduce paperwork and "guidance". It would give heads far more flexibility and freedom of action, for example to set school spending priorities in consultation with teachers and parents. It would recognise value added across many dimensions, so that schools which develop young people from even the most disadvantaged backgrounds are properly celebrated. It would end the present obsession with public examinations. But it would retain enough periodic exams to track progress, however imperfectly, and it would allow new exam alternatives to emerge that are deliberately and publicly tougher than at present.

This approach is a very demanding one. It is demanding on those who work in schools, a minority of whom now may well be happy within the current system of command and control, and will therefore be nervous about new freedoms and new responsibility. It is demanding on government, which must alienate a significant amount of power according to a clear multi-year plan, and then resist attempts to force it to meddle anew. It is demanding on pupils, since the inevitable result of this approach will be that they are encouraged to aspire and to achieve more. And it is demanding on the public, since it requires a high degree of patience and tolerance from them during a process of change.

Much of this line of thought seems to lie behind current educational reform. But notice that all that has really changed is a viewpoint. No policy as such has been adopted here. Nothing has been said about the "Swedish model", about "pupil premiums" or about "supply side reform". The new viewpoint has implications for all of these policy ideas, of course. But the point is that a huge amount of positive reform can be achieved on the basis of common sense and a new perspective, before making what may inevitably be more ideological commitments.

We can use the idea of capability, then, to ground a different set of assumptions about human beings in public policy. Instead of the passive self of orthodox economic theories, we can substitute a positive idea of the active self. We can move, that is, from Theory X to Theory Y.

As we shall see, this implies a radically different conception of what economics is, and so a different analysis of what the fundamental drivers are of economic prosperity, and social well-being. But the immediate point is this: moving to a capabilities approach has the potential to release hitherto unimaginable amounts of social energy, indeed to reinvigorate society as a whole. This is the potential of the Big Society as an idea.

But for it to do so in the face of an over-mighty state requires not merely good government, but appropriate legal protection: a framework of law and culture within which newly empowered individuals and institutions can act. In fact Britain already has such a legal framework. We just need to celebrate it a little more.

8 Law, Liberty and Personal Freedoms

The idea and practice of this political or civil liberty flourish in their highest vigour in these kingdoms, where it falls little short of perfection ... And this spirit of liberty is so deeply implanted in our constitution, and rooted in our very soil, that a slave the moment he lands in England, falls under the protection of the laws, and with regard to all natural rights becomes instantly a freeman.

Sir William Blackstone, **Commentaries on the Laws of England**

In recent years we have become used to news of police raids on crack dens and suspected terrorists. Open fields, however, are another matter. So one can only imagine the bemusement of local residents early on 10 January 2007 when a total of 22 people—10 government officials and 12 police officers—descended secretly and without notice on a remote field in Gloucestershire. They erected a road block and used wire cutters to force their way in, without permission from the owners.

Who was the target of this police "hit"? Not a senior member of Al-Qaeda now living under an alias on a remote English farm, alas.

Not some ram-raiding jewel thieves sitting on a huge stash of swag. No – it was a nine-year old pet Jersey cow named Harriet, which they wrongly suspected of having BSE.

So far we have looked at the economic and political effects of an over-mighty state. Now we turn to its legal effects, of which the growth in state powers to enter the home—there are now more than 1,000 such powers—is but one example. Just as Theory X writes off people as shirkers and forces trust out of society, so intrusive, complex and arbitrary laws undermine our freedoms and our society. In 2006 alone, there were over 5,000 pages of primary legislation or Acts of Parliament, and an additional 11,500 pages of subordinate legislation.

Yet it is not an overstatement to say that the English legal system was founded over time on the diametrically opposite assumption: that personal liberty should be guarded against official interference and that the capabilities of individuals and independent institutions alike should thus be protected. It was founded, that is, on a belief—widespread, unspoken and of great duration—in what we have called the Big Society.

Today, however, this understanding seems to have gone missing. Politicians are squeamish about defending our traditional human rights, the public is often confused about what those rights actually are, and large sections of the media often compound the problem by spreading clear misinformation about them and their effects. Human rights are variously denounced as promoting socialism and state interference, as insinuating a left-wing social agenda into the British legal system, and as impeding the fight against terrorism. There is, as a general rule, little or no truth in these claims.

From the present perspective, moreover, the importance of basic human rights is clear—they are the extension of a belief in human capability into law, and thus a foundation of the Big Society.

Coke and Voltaire

Take the issue of entry powers, for example. The idea that an Englishman's home is his castle was given early expression by Sir Edward Coke, first Lord Chief Justice and framer of the Petition of Right, in *The First Part of the Institutes of the Laws of England* (1628). It was understood then that to cross the threshold of someone's property is to move from a public to what should be a private world, a world in which, broadly, different social conventions, different moral obligations and different legal standards apply. Of course, the state had important reserved rights to enter homes in the public interest, rights that have expanded over time by democratic process, here as in other countries. But over the following three centuries it remained true in Britain that the home was enshrined by law and tradition as a private zone free from state interference—somewhere to drop one's guard, to relax and to enjoy family life.

The position is rather different today. But lest we forget, the case of Harriet the cow was not foreordained. It was not inevitable that we should have ended up with the present over-mighty official bureaucracy, and with ordinary citizens largely unaware of their rights and psychologically unempowered to act on them. Contrast the history of the US, in which the Fourth Amendment to the Constitution briefly and explicitly sets out a prohibition on unreasonable search of private premises and seizure of private property:

> *The right of the people to be secure in their persons, houses, papers, and effects, against unreasonable searches and seizures, shall not be violated, and no Warrants shall issue, but upon probable cause, supported by Oath or affirmation, and par-*

ticularly describing the place to be searched, and the persons or things to be seized.

That amendment was framed in part in reaction to the British Crown's fondness for writs of assistance: open-ended search warrants that were used to search premises for tax purposes. Writs of assistance were abolished in the US by the Fourth Amendment. They remain on the statute book in this country today.

In the 18th century, Britain was celebrated on the continent as the home of the liberty of the individual, of the theatre and the pub, a place where monarchical authority had been made subject to law and freethinkers could dissent more or less without reprisal. So much so that the French *philosophe* Voltaire famously asked, why can't the laws that guarantee British liberties be adopted elsewhere? Today, the question almost sounds ironic.

Yet Voltaire's question had force, because it seemed to many then that the British had definitively answered Hobbes as to who, state or individual, was ultimately in charge. They had answered it in a typically British way, which fudged the status of the individual as between citizen and subject, which deliberately blurred constitutional offices and functions and which filled the space between person and state with a throng of free and independent institutions. But at least they had done so, as the quarrelling powers of Europe had not, and would not for a century (and not always conclusively thereafter). The result was that, like Cromwell's russet-coated Captain, the British knew what they fought for, and loved what they knew.

What they fought for was the rule of law. Not specific laws as such, but the basic principles from which law springs. And respect for individual rights is at the heart of the rule of law.

Edmund Burke and Recorded Rights

Scepticism about human rights is not a new phenomenon. The argument has often been made over the centuries that such rights do not exist but are merely a philosopher's fancy; that they are contrary to the traditions and spirit of the common law; and that politically they infringe the principle of parliamentary sovereignty. After all, was it not Edmund Burke himself who denounced the "rights of man" as harbingers of revolution in his *Reflections on the Revolution in France* (1790), saying "Against these ... rights of men let no government look for security in the length of its continuance, or in the justice and lenity of its administration"?

In fact, however, this objection is the reverse of the truth. In the first place, Burke was not opposed to rights as such, only to "abstract" or "metaphysical" rights. These are rights which have been divorced from a context of legal custom and tradition, rights which mankind is somehow deemed to have enjoyed in an original state of nature. They are uncertain in their full meaning, and potentially revolutionary in their effects.

In sharp contrast to these abstract rights, however, Burke praises "recorded" rights; that is, rights which have been elaborated through the common law. In a crucial but often neglected passage from the *Reflections*, he says:

> *Far am I from denying in theory; full as far is my heart from withholding in practice... the real rights of men... If civil society be made for the advantage of man, all the advantages for which it is made become his right... Whatever each man can separately do, without trespassing upon others, he has a right to*

do for himself; and he has a right to a fair portion of all which society, with all its combinations of skill and force, can do in his favour.

The last two sentences are a masterly statement of Burke's "Old Whig" or "compassionate" conservatism.

So, then: what distinguishes recorded from abstract rights? Simply this: recorded rights are, in effect, summaries of human experience. They are established, they are well-understood, and they have been filtered, elaborated, nuanced and defined in a huge range of different contexts through countless legal judgments. It is in their status as the product of the common law, of the judge-made law of the land, that Burke sees their legitimacy; and in their protection against the tyranny of the majority that he sees their value. From time to time these rights or freedoms may be codified or recorded in statute, and for Burke this is to be welcomed when such a statute operates, in his words, on the principles of the common law.

Thus it is crucial to note that Burke is not opposed to change as such. Far from it: for him acceptance of change is the indispensable corollary of commitment to the established order. As he famously put it "A state without some means of change is without the means of its conservation." Thus, far from reviling the "glorious revolution" of 1688, Burke celebrated it as the necessary and limited change required to preserve the constitution. For him, then, the continuing substance in the body politic—the framework within which any change must occur—is the British constitution, and in particular the common law.

Blackstone, Dicey and the Legal Tradition

Burke would not have considered this line of thought as in any sense innovative, and indeed he would have been appalled at the idea. On the contrary, he regarded himself as writing from within the very heart of British legal, constitutional and specifically parliamentary traditions.

He was correct. For the greatest British legal authorities have always recognised that some basic rights are an essential part of the rule of law. Article 39 of Magna Carta 1215, for example, contains the prohibition "No freemen shall be taken or imprisoned or disseised [sc. expropriated] or exiled or in any way destroyed, nor will we go upon him nor send upon him, except by the lawful judgment of his peers or by the law of the land"—the basis of Articles 5 and 6 of the Human Rights Act today.

Burke's readers would not have needed to look as far back as the 13th century for confirmation of this point, however. For the wider argument had in fact been made very forcefully three decades before the *Reflections*, with the publication of the magisterial *Commentaries on the Laws of England* (1765-9) of Sir William Blackstone.

Blackstone's was the first full-scale presentation of English law, and specifically the common law, for over 200 years. It had three huge merits: it was systematic, presenting the law in a coherent way from first principles; it was written in English, not Latin; and it was aimed not merely at lawyers but at squires, merchants and other educated laymen. It went through eight editions in 11 years, and was vigorously circulated not merely in Britain but in the American colonies. It has had an inestimable influence on the development and spread of the rule of law in the English-speaking world.

For Blackstone, rights are not merely an accretion to the rule of law: they are intrinsic to it. In his words "the principal aim of society is to protect individuals in the enjoyment of those absolute rights, which were invested in them by the immutable laws of nature… Hence it follows, that the primary end of human laws is to maintain and regulate these *absolute* rights of individuals." At the end of the *Commentaries* Blackstone gives a rather Whiggish account of the origins of these rights and liberties, encompassing Magna Carta, the Petition of Right, the Habeas Corpus Acts, the Bill of Rights, and the Act of Settlement. He thus links both Parliament's constitutional function and its own history to the growth of individual freedoms and restraint on the Crown.

In Blackstone's analysis, there are three "absolute" rights: the right to personal security, the right to personal liberty, and the right to private property. These are rights of individuals, not groups, and they are specifically chosen in opposition to different forms of tyranny and oppression. Moreover, they are to be read widely. Thus the right to personal security includes "a person's legal and uninterrupted enjoyment of his life, his limbs, his body, his health and his reputation", while the right to personal liberty includes "the power of removing one's person to whatsoever place one's inclination may direct without imprisonment or restraint, except by due process of law". And Blackstone notably argued that these primary rights were in turn supported and protected by a range of subordinate rights, such as the right of subjects to have access to the courts, and the right of petition. These protections are the forerunner of the modern idea that the law should provide effective remedies.

This broad line of thought was in turn taken up, developed and given a characteristic twist by the great constitutional theorist A V Dicey towards the end of the 19th century. As with Blackstone, Dicey's *Introduction to the Study of the Law of the Constitution* (1885) has been massively influential ever since its first publication.

For Dicey the British constitution rested on two foundations: parliamentary sovereignty and the rule of law. Parliament had unfettered power as the supreme law-making institution. But it was itself held to certain unchanging principles that constituted the rule of law, and these guaranteed the rights and liberties of the individual. These principles were that no-one could be punished except by court order with due process and for a distinct breach of the law; that everyone was subject to law and to the jurisdiction of the courts; and that the general principles of the constitution were derived from judicial decisions in court, that is from judge-made law.

Dicey also emphasises three particular rights: the rights to personal freedom, to freedom of discussion and to public meeting or freedom of association. The latter two are not those of Blackstone, but Blackstone's other rights, to personal security and private property, are clearly assumed elsewhere in Dicey. Where the two theorists differ is that for Dicey these rights, indeed rights as such, have no special status. There are for him no "absolute" or foundational rights. Rights may be well-established, but ultimately they remain the products of judge-made law, of the normal processes of courtroom adjudication. As such they can change: slowly as legal practice evolves, or rapidly through Act of Parliament. For this reason, perhaps, Dicey is generally rather dismissive of formal statements, charters or guarantees of rights: his thought seems to be that if the rights in question are not sufficiently embedded in the law, customs and manners of a nation, then formal guarantees are likely to be of little value.

But Dicey's position is slightly less clear than it might be, for two reasons. The first is the obvious point that formal guarantees may themselves be a way to strengthen the customs and manners of a nation, by recording a public and social commitment to certain basic values. The second point is more subtle: it is that regardless of Dicey's official position there clearly are some rights that he takes to be, if not entrenched, then very well-established indeed—these are the rights assumed in his conception of the rule of law itself, such as the right to due process. A more fully-fledged conception of the rule of law might identify other such rights, and point to them as being wholly or partly constitutive of the rule of law. Parliament would preserve its own unfettered sovereignty, but there would be something self-defeating about the exercise of that sovereignty in the abolition of those basic rights.

What Rights are Not

Unsurprisingly, then, Burke, Blackstone and Dicey share a broadly consistent view of English law and the importance of certain established rights and liberties within it. Not only that: they see it as a primary purpose of government and of the rule of law to protect the liberties of the individual. Good government is maintained by constitutional arrangements that are deliberately slow-moving and yet flexible.

Importantly, none of these thinkers regards the judiciary as anything other than a vital part of our democracy. They recognise that our constitution has evolved so as to embed the power of the executive within that of the legislature, and to balance what results with the independent power of the judiciary.

The power of the judiciary is not merely part of our constitution, however. It is specifically and democratically ratified by Parliament. If the judiciary acts to restrain the power of the executive in some way, it is always open to Parliament, in which the political party or parties of the executive will normally have a majority, to overturn the relevant law or to withdraw from the relevant international convention. Indeed, it is theoretically open to Parliament to repeal all or part of the Act of Settlement 1701, on which the independence of the judiciary formally rests. British democracy thus deliberately constrains itself in order to function more effectively. It sets limits to accountability, and so to the zeal of even the most ardent reforming democrat. The oft-made claim that judges lack legitimacy on the grounds they are not elected thus rests on a misunderstanding. For popular election is not the only source of legitimate public choice, or public power, under the British constitution.

Human rights are sometimes considered to be the product of left-wing ideology. But in Britain at least, this line of thought suggests that the opposite is true. To see why, consider what these rights are not. They are not natural, pre-ordained, or the products of God's law. They belong to individuals, not to groups or classes. They are not, by and large, economic or social in character. They are not divorced from, but are the products of, legal tradition and social custom. They are not conceived of in the abstract or grounded in *a priori* reflection, but based on experience. They are not independent of specific legal remedies, but backed by them. They are not entrenched against Parliament as superior law, but explicitly acknowledge the sovereignty of Parliament.

By contrast, there is a liberal or radical conception of human rights in which they are all or many of these things. The French revolution was founded on such a conception, and part of Burke's genius was to predict in advance that, and how, such a revolution would end in disaster. But the American revolution is arguably a more interesting case, because it allied radical rhetoric in the style of Thomas Paine with radical innovation in its entrenched and written constitution, and specifically the Bill of Rights, and then grafted the whole onto English legal traditions directly and recently inspired by Blackstone himself. From this rich and heady mixture came, in the course of a century, not merely the extraordinary energy of American statecraft, but a powerful and distinct conception of national identity, of what it was to be American at all.

The Politics of Human Rights

The British tradition of human rights is based, then, on centuries of casework in which personal freedoms have been set out and protected against official intervention through the common law. How does this history bear on current politics?

The first thing to note is that the deep tension that now exists between different traditions on both right and left in British politics. On the broad left, radical preachers sought to use common-law protection of individual freedoms to argue for religious toleration and freedom to worship in Britain for over three hundred years. The guild socialist tradition drew on the same framework of rights to establish and build a huge network of independent institutions supporting working men and women throughout the 19th and early 20th centuries.

But it was of course the Fabian tradition, with its belief in the powers of the state, which eventually trumped the others. The result has been that the left has increasingly demanded a much more activist kind of rights culture. It has not been satisfied with political solutions to problems of poverty and inequality, but has sought to extend the realm of rights into so-called socio-economic rights, such as a right to work. It has sought to treat as fundamental rights a whole host of subordinate and politically contested legal powers granted over the years by government. But at the same time it also emphasised a fundamentally collectivist view of rights, placing primary emphasis on the state or the "common good".

Finally, the focus of the left has been less on means than on ends, and on subsuming legal procedure and existing rights beneath the quest for social justice. At its most utopian, this view holds that any institution—national or local, public or private—is potentially available to be used to pursue social goals. Thus even the integrity of the judicial system itself is of interest only insofar as it serves to secure equality of outcomes and to enforce social justice. In Oakeshott's phrase, human society becomes an "enterprise association": made subject to some overriding purpose which takes priority over private interests and which stands ready to sacrifice individual freedom for the greater good. In such a society the rule of law is always at risk.

These tensions explain the deeply conflicted view of different Labour Prime Ministers to the European Convention on Human Rights and its counterpart within British law, the Human Rights Act. Both documents contain a list of carefully drafted rights which ultimately derive, with the exception of the right to privacy, from the English common law. Yet the post-war Labour Prime Minister Clement Attlee was suspicious of the European Convention and supported it with reluctance, while Tony Blair and Jack Straw, who were swift to introduce the Human Rights Act after the 1997 election, in due course became angry critics of the Act. On issues of law and order and security, Prime Minister Blair believed in a strong, powerful and centralised state, as we have seen. The Act hindered his government from carrying out some of its most populist and authoritarian policies.

By contrast, the conservative vision of law is, broadly, a procedural one. Conservatives insist that the rules should be observed, wherever they may lead. They attend to history. They try to be fastidious in distinguishing between and attending to the specific character of different institutions. They demand impartiality of administration, equality of access to justice and a ban on special treatment. For them the proper means to address public issues of social inequality is through democratic politics. Individual freedom is preserved through the rule of law, backed by the state as final enforcer. Human society moves further towards a "civil association": a group of people who agree to subject themselves to a set of common rules of conduct, so that they can better pursue their own various lives and interests with as little interference as possible.

What, then, of the Conservative party? As we have seen, the strength of the party as a political movement has often derived from an energizing tension between different principles, a tension which is intrinsic to conservatism itself. Nowhere is this clearer than in its attitude to human rights. On the one hand the mainstream party has consistently adhered to the ancient and liberal tradition of British scepticism about the role and extent of the state. On the other, there is also a tradition of Conservative respect for authority, which can sometimes elevate the state above the rights and liberties of individuals.

This latter strand of thinking has received fresh impetus since 9/11. The logic can seem compelling: the first duty of the state is to protect its citizens; global terrorism poses a potentially existential threat to British citizens; so any measures by the state are legitimate to combat this threat. The argument is given rhetorical potency by the language of warfare, with its implicit suggestion that normal constitutional arrangements are to be set aside.

There is little need to rehearse the arguments on this issue, beyond three obvious remarks. The first is that very serious terrorist threats are not new. Lest we forget, the Gunpowder Plot of 1605 was designed to kill both the monarch and his successor and the entire political and ecclesiastical leadership of this country. The second is that this country is not in a state of emergency. In an emergency, the supreme necessity of survival creates an imperative for action. Rightly or wrongly, various leaders including Pitt and Lincoln have even thought it necessary to suspend *habeas corpus* in order to protect the life of the nation and the government itself in the most difficult possible circumstances. But those circumstances are not, or not yet, those of today. The third is that the curtailment of individual liberties should be not the first but the last resort for government. Of course, as Mark Twain said, when all you have is a hammer everything looks like a nail. But it is quite clear that the Blair-Brown government in particular was far too ready to reach for legislation to fight terror, in this area as in every other, rather than do the job properly and well.

But the real point is this: that in its modern form, this authoritarian strand is hardly a form of conservatism at all. Rather, it is rationalist. Ultimately, this line of thought would put at risk both the freedom of our institutions and the rule of law itself.

Law and Identity

The British human rights tradition is, then, a reflection within our law of a deep belief in human capability and the importance of personal freedom. It has always been intrinsically small-c conservative. As judge-made law it has proceeded by degrees. As statute in the Human

Rights Act it respects the sovereignty of Parliament. It is, as Burke was, rightly sceptical of the status and value of abstract, "metaphysical" rights.

As the product of a slowly building consensus, this broader tradition has long transcended party politics. It is not, however, neutral between different political viewpoints. On the left, it is generally hostile to Fabian socialism and the growth of state powers; on the right, to any authoritarian strand within the Conservative party. It is hostile to attempts to introduce new socio-economic and other rights, which generally have little if any grounding in our law or practice. And it is thus a foundation stone of a connected or Big society.

It also has deep implications for how we see ourselves. Of course, different people will have different views about the very idea of a British national identity. But this is as it should be. The point is not to trade intuitions about what is or is not authentically British, but to note the consequences of this line of thought for reflection on our culture and identity.

In that spirit it encourages us to understand, however unfashionable it may be to do so, that even today there is something extraordinary and distinctive about Great Britain and its island story. This is a matter not of any God-given right to rule but of our language, of our institutions, and of the example we can set to ourselves and to others. *Il y a encore une certaine idée de la Grande Bretagne*, to paraphrase General de Gaulle. This is not cause for complacency, nor for self-depreciation or condescension. It is simply how we are, a way in which many others see us, and something for us to live up to if we can.

We are accustomed to think of democracy as the supreme expression of human self-governance. But as Hobbes reminds us, the most fundamental such achievement is in fact the rule of law, since without the rule of law no government can take place at all. And historically, this country enjoyed the rule of law, to greater or lesser degree, for around nine hundred years before the creation of a full democracy in the modern sense. It is the fundamental institution in which we as a nation are invested, and by which we have been formed.

Again following Hobbes, we are apt to think of law as requiring a sovereign to enforce it. But this need not be so. A people may be so bound by its own collective sense of identity as to feel constitutively obliged to obey its own laws, even where no external enforcement exists. Obeying the law can simply be part of its identity. Arguably, this is now true of the Jewish diaspora. It may also be true of Britain that respect for the law, and indeed respect for other traditional values, is partly constitutive of what it is to be British. Any derogation from these values in foreign or domestic policy would then be, to that extent at least, an erasing of what it is to be us: a kind of suicide.

If this is true, it would help to explain the peculiarly anguished nature of the public debate over the invasion of Iraq, for example. But it would also have a direct impact on British relations with Islam more generally. For many Muslims are, it seems, bound in a somewhat similar way by their adherence to Sharia law, wherever in the world they may be. The stage is thus set for possible conflict between the British sovereign demand for obedience to civil authority, and the constitutive requirement on traditional Muslims, including of course those in Britain, to obey the Sharia. The point is not to be alarmist; it is simply to note the broad similarity of the commitment on each side.

Finally, there is a more specific source for concern. It is well known that many of the powers of Parliament have been ceded over time to the European Union, or constrained by international law and treaty. Nevertheless it remains true that in England and Wales (matters are arguably slightly different for Scotland) a democratically elected government can—in principle at least and provided it is sufficiently persistent—make or amend any law by a simple parliamentary majority in the House of Commons.

This flexibility is an important aspect of the British constitution. Yet, from the present standpoint, it also creates a deep problem. If the state continues to grow, executive power increases and constitutional safeguards decline—if the UK becomes ever more an enterprise society—then it is inevitable that the status of the rule of law itself must increasingly come under threat. With no formally entrenched basic law, and in the face of weakening respect by government for constitutional conventions that have historically had the force of law, the question is simply this: on what long-term basis is the rule of law itself to be upheld?

The answer can only be: on what we understand about ourselves, and our traditions and values; that is, on our sense of identity as a nation. If this is correct, then further reflection on British identity and British institutions is both required and potentially extremely valuable, as we shall see. The next chapter also looks at how British culture and the idea of human capability expressed through free institutions can support the Big Society—but in the sphere of business.

9 **Institutions, Competition and Entrepreneurship**

Economics is the study of mankind in the ordinary business of life.
Alfred Marshall

The great dialectic in our time is not, as anciently and by some still supposed, between capital and labour; it is between economic enterprise and the state.
J. K. Galbraith

The Napoleonic Wars were won in 1688. Before the reader leaps to denounce this obvious error, let us acknowledge that Napoleon himself was finally defeated at Waterloo in 1815. Nevertheless, the basic cause of his defeat was the bloodless arrival of William III on the British throne 127 years earlier. That event established three pillars of economic success, which supported British society—and British naval power—for more than 200 years. Those pillars remain fundamental to the Big Society today.

How so? During the 17th century, it will be recalled, Great Britain experimented unsuccessfully with three different forms of government: by the monarch under the periods of personal rule of James I and, in particular, Charles I; by parliament, briefly after the Civil War; and by the army under Oliver Cromwell. The Restoration of the monarchy in 1660 created an increasingly uneasy truce between these forces. This truce was ridden out by Charles II, but ultimately resulted in the enforced exile of the catholic James II and the arrival of the Protestant Stadtholder of the Netherlands as William III.

William's arrival was an event of enormous political and religious importance, of course. But it also had huge economic significance. Under the new constitutional order, sovereignty now lay not with the King as such, but with the "King-in-Parliament". The King was enabled to hold executive power, especially in matters of defence, but only as constrained by parliament. The effect of this was to discipline the public finances.

Before 1688, British monarchs regularly needed revenue, both to fund their own courts and to fight wars. But they were reluctant to do so through taxation, since this meant calling a parliament, and parliaments inevitably sought new rights and privileges from the Crown. Accordingly, hard-up monarchs had long raised funds by selling off titles and Crown estates, by creating and selling the rights to artificial monopolies such as in tobacco, and by "forced loans" from nobles and London bankers. Each had serious drawbacks: titles became devalued; selling off estates meant the Crown had a smaller and smaller revenue base, which merely compounded the original problem; artificial monopolies pushed prices up and inhibited trade; and forced loans were a form of gentlemanly extortion and were rarely repaid.

After 1688 all this changed. Because the new monarch had less power, he was more trustworthy. Parliament would not allow William to default, and so his promises to repay loans suddenly became credible. The result was that Crown indebtedness rose from £1 million in 1688 to almost £17 million in 1697. Interest rates fell to reflect the new security of the loans, from 14% in the early 1690s to 6-8% before 1700, and only 3% by the 1720s. Much of the new money was spent on the War of the Spanish Succession, in which the Duke of Marlborough won his great victories in the first decade of the new century.

William's arrival also released a huge wave of new ideas, including Dutch business practices and financial expertise. The first long-term loan was made in 1693, and the Bank of England was founded in 1694. Credit was increasingly available for adventurous British entrepreneurs and traders, and a world of commercial opportunities lay before them. The result was to make Britain by far the most prosperous and successful nation in the world for almost two hundred years.

France had long been the one great continental superpower under Louis XIV. But her autocratic and personal monarchy, rigid and centralised administration and inert parliament created a weak system of government. She lacked the openness, trust and free institutions to generate a large entrepreneur class and above all, she lacked credit, since the government defaulted repeatedly on its debts. When the Napoleonic Wars came to be fought, Britain had enjoyed interest rates some 4-7% below French rates for decades. It had used its astonishing access to capital to re-equip and copper-bottom the Royal Navy, among other things, and sea power was to prove a crucial factor in the struggle against Napoleon. Indeed, the Navy was able to sustain a policy of having more fighting vessels than the rest of the world combined for most of the 19th century. Thus did a constitutional change in 1688 underwrite military success in 1815.

Introducing I-C-E

This brief venture into history is a case study of the Big Society in action. But it is also a huge cautionary tale. It perfectly illustrates the long-term dangers of our present system of government writ large. France failed in the 18th century because it was subject to a central-ised, autocratic and personal government, which was not constrained by parliament or disciplined by competing sources of power. Britain succeeded because it was flexible, free and enterprising, massively open to new ideas, and possessed of a balanced constitution and a well-grounded rule of law.

These are precisely the foundations of economic success today. We can think of them under the headings I-C-E: Institutions, Competi-tion and Entrepreneurship. Conventional economics has remarkable difficulty in dealing coherently with these important ideas. But we will look at them rather differently.

However, it is important to note up-front that these economic foundations were and are as much social as economic. By the early 19th century Britain had not merely the strongest economy, but in many ways the strongest society of any major European state. Per capita income was by far the highest in Europe. Poverty was in general far less widespread and less deep than elsewhere. British levels of literacy and numeracy dwarfed those of France and the continent. And these social strengths were vital to her success, in warfare as in business.

Needless to say, the point is not that we should abolish the welfare state and return to the Poor Laws. Nor is it that a free economy and a free society always go together; they need not, at least in the short run. But the two are inseparably joined in Britain. We have learned the lesson that all economic policy has social implications. We now need to relearn the converse lesson: the foundations of our economic prosperity are social foundations. Thus the way to a stronger economy in Britain lies in part through social renewal.

Institutions

Within this political viewpoint, as we have already seen, independent institutions play an absolutely fundamental role. Constitutionally, they promote good order, restrain excessive power and protect the basic freedoms of the citizen. But they also give shape and meaning to our lives: they command our loyalty and affection, and they help to define us and shape our identity. Finally, they are the repositories of much human wisdom and knowledge, embodying the collective experience of previous generations, experience which can and frequently does outstrip the wisdom of those who would reform them.

The significance of this line of thought is that in place of a simple opposition between the individual and the state, it substitutes a three-way relationship between individuals, institutions and the state. It is when this relationship is functioning well that societies flourish. This requires each element in the triad to be active and energised in its own right. But when it is, then each imposes a constraint and a discipline on the other two. It holds them more accountable. It forces them to do more, to converse with each other, and the whole becomes stronger.

Economically, we can think of institutions as all settled arrangements, formal and informal, which facilitate the exchange of goods and services. They can be utterly abstract or very concrete: they can be rules, customs, traditions, and practices, or they can be fish markets and car boot sales. They can be specifically instituted by private or public action, or they can simply arise. They can be IBM, or they can be money. The economic importance of institutions such as a trusted common currency, readily available credit, secure property rights, and an established and enforceable law of contract has long been known. But of course the importance of intangible norms and conventions and "nudges" may be no less great.

The effect of adopting an institutional perspective is to restore to policy-making many of the elements that are purged by the conventional approach. The world of conventional economics is arid, impersonal and atemporal. The institutional world, however, is fantastically diverse, richly peopled and heavily influenced by the past. It restores, indeed it has built into it, a presumption against one-size-fits-all thinking. And it places a higher burden on government to justify state action, which must inevitably disrupt existing institutions, social networks and shared knowledge.

Competition

Economic institutions and individuals often co-operate with each other. But they also compete. Indeed, it seems to be a deep part of human nature and human culture to do both.

Some people regard competition and markets as intrinsically bad, in the belief that they put people into rivalry with each other and feed off and so encourage emotions of greed and fear. As we have noted, there is certainly a problem when a narrowly economic conception of human good and human values leaches back into society as such. And there is a further problem when policymakers, under the influence of standard *rigor mortis* economics, forget that markets are culturally created and sustained and adopt a purely laissez-faire approach.

But as an economic matter, it should not need saying that competition and markets are absolutely vital to society's well-being. This is not just because of their role in resource allocation and wealth generation. On the contrary, well-functioning markets are the greatest tool of basic economic development ever created. Competitive prices tend to be low prices, which help the poor and the economically unwary, and markets have made a huge difference to many of the poorest nations on Earth. And finally, markets are tools of communication and exchange, which put people in touch with each other who may otherwise have no affinity—religious, social or ethnic—with each other at all. They are in this sense a source, not of social breakdown, but of social cohesion.

On the deeper issues, however, we again need a shift in perspective. Recall that in the conventional economic world, competition is understood as a state. "Perfect competition" is a virtual state of affairs in which everything—prices, quantities, products—is settled and fixed. There is no change, so there is no scope for discovery or learning. Most importantly, by thinking of people as mere economic agents, this approach treats them simply as passive recipients and not as dynamic forces for change.

When government economists and politicians adopt this static view, the effect is to inhibit them from seeing markets as evolving processes which change over time. The question becomes not "Can we really understand what is going on here?" but automatically leaps to "How can this state of affairs be improved?" or "What can government do to help?" And so the door is opened to all kinds of ill-advised state intervention and rationalist planning.

But this is wrong-headed. Competition is not static but dynamic. It can be cut-throat or moderate, and it can wax or wane. Markets are evolutionary, transient and sometimes semi-chaotic. Generally unpredictable, they are often driven by fashion or group-think. And not all markets are the same. Some are deep, resilient and slow to change, while others are shallow, jumpy and apt to clog up easily. Sometimes the same markets change their basic character over time, depending on who is active in them. Just look at the world's financial markets in 2007-9.

Again, then, one-size-fits-all solutions are bound to fail. Consider our schools once more. Any good teacher knows that children naturally both compete and co-operate. The idea that competition can somehow be eliminated from schools by government fiat is simple nonsense. And it is also profoundly misguided, since competition is a means, one among many, to encourage people of any age to improve their capabilities, and far too many young people leave school today with little to show for their time there.

But competition has limits. You can have competition for which a child is not ready—competition which is too narrow or too intense. There are many areas of human capability and attainment, and so of school life, where competition is hardly relevant at all. And different schools have different values and characters. In other words, competition in schools is inevitable, dynamic and manageable. How to manage it, is a judgement call. Only good heads and good teachers—and certainly not government—can make that call successfully.

The rejection of one-size-fits-all solutions cuts both ways, however. It can also apply to libertarians such as those who adopt the one-size view that more choice is always good. Take the market for baked beans. It does not take the average student long to trawl down a supermarket shelf in the first week of term and figure out what the different baked bean options are, how much they cost, and what extra value he gets from larger packs or buying own-brand. He can, if he wishes, buy beans every week for a term or a year. In this case wide choice is good. It is hard even to imagine a decent case for further regulation.

But what about the markets for mortgages or car insurance? These are rare or one-off purchases, in which people systematically mistake what is in their financial best interest. Mistakes are typically very expensive. And the decisions involved can be fantastically complex and hard to optimise. Indeed, some of the main suppliers may gain from the complexity, if purchasers are unwilling or unable to shop around endlessly. Here the case for regulation to simplify and standardise the different alternatives in the market—and so restrict choice—is much stronger. People are not economic androids, after all.

The point is that too much choice can itself inhibit good decision-making. Pensions and other retirement plans are almost always financially good for you due to tax breaks and other subsidies. But a recent study of 800,000 employees in America showed that the larger the number of retirement plans they were offered, the less likely it was that they would join any plan at all. In some countries, too, the government itself is forcing people to make private decisions about savings or healthcare. In cases like these, it can make good sense—it can enable human freedom rather than restricting it—to have a smaller number of basic choices, plus an opt-out for those who regard themselves as genuine experts.

Entrepreneurship

The last of our three foundations is entrepreneurship. The normal picture of an entrepreneur might be of an Alan Sugar or an Anita Roddick; that is, a successful businessman or woman who has made millions from a brilliant idea. On this view, entrepreneurs are unusually bright, or driven, or nervy. They go to business school or have science PhDs. Capitalism is about capital, and the reason why it needs entrepreneurs is because they create the capital.

Within our received economic theory, however, entrepreneurs do not exist as such at all. Not only that: they cannot exist. All markets are deemed to be in equilibrium, so there are no free lunches and no unexploited opportunities. For the same reason, there can be no competition, and prices never move. In this world, don't forget, nothing ever happens.

The standard view thus makes it all but impossible for government to understand entrepreneurs and entrepreneurship. Entrepreneurship is a necessary, vital, chaotic, unpredictable and creative process. And as such it is a process that is generally beyond state control, however much governments talk about it and try to foster it. Typically governments ignore or underplay the negative impact of new policy initiatives on existing businesses; as we saw earlier with friendly societies. Or they grossly overestimate the effect of new spending on entrepreneurial activity; as with the Treasury's many ineffective direct attempts to improve private sector productivity and rates of innovation. Or they fund some semi-oxymoronic attempt at state entrepreneurship directly.

Yet the conventional view of an entrepreneur is not quite right either. Entrepreneurs are not always unusually bright or driven. If they were, there would be a lot fewer of them around and Great Britain would be a lot poorer than it is. A better way to think of entrepreneurship is as a kind of alertness to opportunity. On this view, entrepreneurship is 90% the discovery of a hidden cost. The entrepreneur might be the inventor of the mobile phone. It might be an importer of silks to the UK. But it might also be the house-husband who stretches a limited budget further by walking down to CostCo for his bulk purchases.

Such a wide definition might seem meaningless. But the point is precisely that entrepreneurship is everywhere. It is not a business activity so much as one aspect of the ceaselessly interesting and creative nature of human beings. And it implies that, far from always being in equilibrium, markets are hardly ever in any kind of meaningful equilibrium. Writers, for example, used quills until the late 19th century. Since then they have used fountain pens, the typewriter, the electric typewriter, the dot-matrix printer, the inkjet printer, the laser printer and the colour laser printer. In other words, the market kept on changing as alert entrepreneurs noticed what hidden costs and unsatisfied needs were out there and how they could be newly met. Who knows what will come next?

On this view, too, there is nothing about entrepreneurship that requires entrepreneurs to have capital of their own. Rather, what matters is imagination — the ability to spot or conceive opportunities — and a willingness to take risks. If the opportunity is good enough, then the capital will normally be available. Indeed, the possession of capital of one's own may and often does reduce entrepreneurship, by reducing the appetite for risk.

The significance of the I-C-E perspective here is thus threefold. First, it is egalitarian. Successful business entrepreneurs rightly deserve to be honoured for their role in wealth creation. But entrepreneurs are not a special class, and market processes are not intrinsically biased towards the haves over the have-nots. There are no particular barriers of knowledge or wealth or background that prevent us all from being highly entrepreneurial if we choose, and it is this wider energy that underwrites our prosperity.

Secondly, I-C-E reminds us that entrepreneurship is not just about business. It is embedded in society, and some of the greatest entrepreneurship in the UK is to be found in not-for-profit organisations, and in co-operatives — all the more so since they generally have limited capital reserves.

And finally, it highlights the limits of government intervention yet again. Indeed, it suggests that an educational culture which is slanted towards business and other strictly "relevant" subjects may be blinkered and misconceived. The idea of entrepreneurship as a kind of alertness implies that what we need from our schools is not pre-packaged little businesspeople or workers as such, but generalists with open, inquiring and wide-ranging minds. Now that's a revolutionary thought.

Co-ops, Mutualism and Employee Ownership

The I-C-E perspective thus takes things we think we already understand, like competition and entrepreneurship, and looks at them in a new and rather different way. It is highly unorthodox. Indeed, it is sceptical about the very idea of orthodoxy. As a result, it can encourage us to look more carefully at some apparently obvious and standard ideas, and to rehabilitate ideas that have hitherto seemed unavailable.

This is exactly what it does with co-ops, mutuals and employee-owned companies. Traditionally, these organisations have been regarded in Britain as intrinsically left-wing. In this often rather Marxist view politics is really about the struggle between labour and capital, and it has been the historic function of the political left to uphold the interests of labour, and of the right those of capital. Moreover, co-ops, mutuals and employee-owned companies have no outside shareholders to supply capital, as firms do. So how can they be in any sense capitalist institutions?

Yet if we step back from these standard views, it becomes evident that co-ops are in many respects—hold onto your hat—a rather conservative, indeed capitalist, idea.

A co-op is a form of organisation in which, very crudely, control is distributed not one share-one vote, as in a company, but one member-one vote. This gives it an intrinsically democratic character. It makes it hard to raise external capital, and it means a co-op always needs strong leadership, on pain of becoming a talking shop. But it also makes co-ops extremely stimulating, energising and often entrepreneurial places to work. Similar things are true of other shared ownership organisations, including employee-owned companies, credit unions and mutual societies.

The first successful co-op in the world was established by the Rochdale Pioneers, in 1844. They were 28 poor weavers and tradesmen looking for a better future as the industrial revolution mechanised the cloth trade. The co-op was in fact their third attempt to set up for themselves. The first, in 1830, failed due to lack of capital. The second, in 1843, relied on employers making a modest contribution but came unstuck when many refused to pay up.

The third, in the following year, relied on slowly accumulated subscriptions of £1 each from the members, and initially made a modest £13 a week in sales. By 1850, however, the co-op had 600 members, £2,299 in capital, and sales of £300 a week. In 1861, it diversified into housing for its members. By the end of the 19th century, it had established the Co-operative Building Society, a major provider of mortgages.

But look at the pioneers' experience again. Their success was the result of self-help, entrepreneurship and community energy—the virtues of a Big Society—not state patronage and official intervention. They were able to adapt the co-operative form and the broader idea of shared ownership to a variety of social needs: a local food shop, local housing and local mortgages. And they were motivated as much by high ideals and a rich conception of human good as by economic necessity: after all, in their very first year of operation, they published the Rochdale Principles, to which all co-ops broadly adhere today.

Exactly these things are needed today if we are to combat the increasing fragmentation of British society. The present social recession demands a considered but radical programme of change. This includes rebalancing power away from the state and further towards the individual through constitutional reform and deregulation. It includes devolving more power from Whitehall to local government and a relocalisation of public services. And it also includes breathing new life into old institutional forms … such as co-ops. Co-ops are thus not just the latest Conservative idea du jour. They are a clear and important extension of the overall Big Society project.

Food makes the point perfectly. At present the UK food industry is dominated by the view that the only priority is low prices at the till. As a result we have cheap food of amazing variety and abundance. All well and good—except that we also have failing high streets, high food miles, artificially low prices to the farmer, increased car and petrol usage to out-of-town shops, lower food security, and a widespread popular ignorance of what food is and where it comes from.

Local food co-ops, by contrast, by-pass the supermarkets. They support local growers and provide good affordable food. They protect the environment. And they build local communities, not an impersonal retail monoculture. If you don't believe it, look at the Park Slope co-op in New York, which has 12,000 members, a 75% volunteer work force—since all members must work in the co-op—and a 20%+ discount on food prices to members. That's a prize worth fighting for.

As with food, so the potential for co-ops and related institutions to be used in such disparate areas as housing, adult and children's social care, health care, education, the benefits system, agriculture, the arts has barely been tapped. What unites these different activities is that they are all heavily reliant on human capital. Co-ops tap human energy and capability, and so naturally generate human capital. They bring those involved closer to their clients, customers, users or patients. They substitute the human touch for red tape and impersonality.

And they allow us to pinpoint once again what has gone wrong with the Labour party. Under Tony Blair the Labour government started fairly well in this area, with the establishment of a Co-operative Commission led by John Monks, which reported in 2001. After that very little of any real substance or energy happened at all. One need not be a professional cynic to see the Commission as a token gesture to co-operative enthusiasts on the left, including the Co-operative political party which, lest we forget, still funds and supports 28 Labour MPs including Ed Balls. Once that gesture had been made, the party's dominant Fabian belief in the state duly reasserted itself.

The present situation is thus replete with irony. Britain invented the co-operative movement, and was an earlier pioneer in mutualism and employee ownership. Yet it has some of the lowest relative usage of co-ops in Europe, and lower too than in the USA. Politically, the early Labour party was able to draw on a strong co-operative and mutual tradition, yet after taking power in 1997 it largely ignored that tradition. For its part, the British co-operative movement has long aligned itself with Labour. Yet this linkage is an historical accident: co-ops are not intrinsically of either the left or right, and there is no reason in principle why the co-operative movement should not be supporting MPs from other parties. Perhaps it is time it was asked to do so.

Finally, co-ops illustrate again the deeper issue we have raised about the nature of the individual. Are humans most fulfilled when they are active or passive? Is human happiness purely a matter of mental states, of the reception of pleasant sensory inputs, or is it a matter of personal engagement and personal achievement?

Co-ops are no panacea. But within this argument, they fall squarely on the side of the active individual. As with any entrepreneurial organisation, they involve risk and the commitment of capital, energy and love. But more than this, they do not merely cater to people as consumers, but often make demands on them as members. Their flat ownership structures give them an intrinsically democratic character, and an often robust internal debate. And they operate within a clear ethical framework set out by the Rochdale principles. All of which stand as a corrective to the passivity which politicians and economists too often assume to be the keynote of our human nature.

Two Worries

A Big Society approach to economic renewal thus stresses I-C-E, and the huge potential for independent institutions such as co-ops, mutuals and shared ownership organisations to make a difference in both the private and public sectors.

But at this point, the reader may be feeling rather perplexed. Where are the usual economic policy soundbites? What's happened to tax cuts, fiscal policy, the rolling back of the state, or any of the other supposed staples of centre-right thinking on economics? What does this view have to say about monetary and fiscal policy? The discussion so far doesn't feel like it has had anything much to do with economic policy at all.

This is as it should be. The present argument is not about economic policy as such, or even new economic ideas. It is about how we understand the fundamental drivers of our prosperity. Its goal is to question our basic assumptions about economics, and to contribute to the new, compassionate conservative viewpoint of which the Big Society is an expression.

Any well-considered new viewpoint naturally generates new ideas. And as we shall see later, I-C-E is extremely radical and fertile in its policy implications. But this in turn generates a further worry. It's all very well to criticise our conventional economics, one might think. But that economics is massively widely studied in our universities, it is a well-organised and well-understood body of theory, and it is supported by a large amount of empirical work. Where is the intellectual backing for all this I-C-E guff?

This criticism misses the target. There is a wide gap between the economics that is practised in British government today, and the frontiers of the subject in academia. Academic economists are only too aware of this, and of the limitations of their discipline, as we have noted. They are aware of the profound difference between the descriptive study of economics and the normative process of recommending and implementing changes to policy on the ground. And they are aware of the rather poor record of academic economists in making useful economic predictions.

The real problem lies not within the academy, as we have seen, but in how economics is (mis)understood within politics, within public administration and within society. We need to break the present stale monopoly, open up public debate to new ways of thinking, and give policymakers new scope and new licence to think creatively about possible solutions. That opening-up of debate is far more important than any particular contribution to the debate itself.

In fact, however, the I-C-E perspective does not lack intellectual rigour. In technical terms, it is a blend of institutional, behavioural and

Austrian economics. Each of these has its own history, its own body of academic research and ideas, and its own respected proponents.

Nor does the present approach lack evidence. On the contrary, it is supported by a large and increasing body of academic research, some of which is cited in the Endnotes. It helps to explain large parts of Britain's historic prosperity, as we have already seen. And it can also go some way to explain more recent events. The relative fortunes of Germany and the UK since the Second World War, for example, have been closely geared to how much emphasis each has placed on maintaining free and independent institutions, orderly markets and conditions of economic freedom in which individual entrepreneurship can succeed.

The fall of communism in Eastern Europe and Russia can also be understood in these terms. In effect these countries suffered a triple failure, which dispelled trust and marginalised society: virtually no free and independent institutions, hardly any genuine competition and little (legal) entrepreneurship.

The countries that have flourished since 1989 have been those in which these three elements have been re-established and re-grounded in existing traditions and folk memories. And the record of Western technical advisers in assisting the transition from Communism to capitalism has been an extremely mixed one, precisely because they have often promoted a foolish economic orthodoxy that ignored both local circumstances and these fundamental drivers of prosperity. They forgot what made their own societies, and economies, big in the first place.

10 **The New Conservatism**

The men who create power make an indispensable contribution to the Nation's greatness, but the men who question power make a contribution just as indispensable, especially when that questioning is disinterested, for they determine whether we use power or power uses us.

John F. Kennedy

Let us briefly take stock. The British economy and British society are not well. A central reason for this is the growth in the size and pervasiveness of the state. Having tested to destruction the idea of the state as a cure for social ills, the Fabian left has little if anything left to say. But equally the two dominant Conservative traditions of paternalism and libertarianism seem inadequate to the problem: the first because it lacks a critique of the state, the second because it lacks a critique of the market.

However, the new Big Society or compassionate conservatism offers a way forward. It addresses both sides of the argument, social and economic, in a fresh and compelling way. It offers a new vision of society based on first principles, by rethinking some of our most fundamental political assumptions. It matches this with an analysis of human well-being and motivation that is sharply at odds with the conventional economic wisdom. And it extends that analysis into a renewed emphasis on the true but neglected drivers of economic prosperity: institutions, competition and entrepreneurship.

At once, however, a host of questions arises. What is this new conservatism? Where does it come from? Why should anyone believe it?

Three Challenges

There are three particular challenges that need to be addressed. The first claims that the present compassionate conservatism is essentially the same as that promoted by George W. Bush before and during his first term as US President. In fact, however, Bush's compassionate conservatism has virtually nothing to do with the ideas we are discussing. It suffered from the twin drawbacks of being neither compassionate nor conservative. It was not compassionate: indeed, its main promoter John DiIulio fell foul of his colleagues in the White House by insisting that money be directed to black and Latino churches, thus alienating white Evangelicals. And it was not conservative, as was shown by the extension of federal influence into local schools through the No Child Left Behind Act of 2002, and the extraordinary ramp up in federal spending that took place even before the financial crash of 2008. Moreover, Bush's compassionate conservatism was a moralising doctrine, which assumed that society's basic moral standards were in decline and set the federal government the task of improving them. Finally, as a slogan, Bush's "compassionate conservatism" lacked a deeper theoretical justification that could be used as a basis for long-term policymaking. It quickly came to seem merely an electoral expedient, not a genuine contribution to a wider political and cultural debate.

The compassionate conservatism that we are discussing provides the wider political context for the Big Society, and it is quite different. It has a strong ethical basis, as we shall see. But it is not a moralising strand of ideas, and does not in general regard the moral character of British society as fit subject for legislation. Indeed it explicitly repudiates such a view in its critique of "enterprise society", something that also sets compassionate conservatism apart from many communitarian views. It does not lack a moral sense, but it locates moral responsibility primarily at the level of the individual, not at that of the state or institution. And consistent with this, its idea of compassion is not that of pity but of com-passion or fellow-feeling—what Adam Smith called "sympathy": one of identification, concern and empathy with others, not of condescension to them. At root, this derives from the same insight as that behind the connected society.

There are two further and related challenges: call them the "old left" and the "new left" challenges. The old left challenge is well-known and widely held: the idea of compassionate conservatism is an oxymoron, a contradiction in terms. On this view, conservatism is about unleashing people's basest instincts: a greed for material possessions and a fear of losing social and economic advantage. It uses markets to set people against one another, and these markets do not cure social injustice and poverty but create and perpetuate them. Conservatism is thus ideologically opposed to compassion, whatever "compassion" amounts to. In the face of this, only the state has the power and the social opportunity to stand up for people against the market.

The new left challenge is more subtle, a reflection of post-democratic politics. It simply says: we've been here before. This is just political posturing. There is a centre ground in British politics, which Thatcher redefined and Blair then occupied. Compassionate conservatism is just a vague cliché, another move in the power game, an attempt to revive a dying brand and identify a line of intellectual succession from Thatcher to Blair to Cameron which is rhetorically predisposed to favour the Tories. It is not an intellectually distinctive set of ideas. Nothing genuine or new is happening here.

The new left challenge can go further: it can claim that compassionate conservatism is just communitarian thinking in disguise. Many centre-left intellectuals, especially in the US where Fabianism is less strong, have long acknowledged that markets may be beneficent and big government deeply problematic. Indeed, American academics such as Robert Putnam and Amitai Etzioni have explored the crowding-out effects that state action can have on civil society. This provides further reason to think compassionate conservatism can have nothing new to say. And if it could, the challenge continues, if there were indeed a need to rein in the state so as to advance social justice, then this is a task that we should only entrust to those who have credibility to manage both the state and social justice; that is, the left.

We can now see that both challenges are wrong: the first, because it rests on a caricature of economic liberalism that we have already rejected; the second because it underestimates the philosophical depth and coherence of the tradition we have described, and the present intellectual bankruptcy of the left as such.

Religious, Fraternal and Civil Strands

The new conservatism is thus distinct, humane and substantive. It is recognisably conservative in its scepticism about the power of the state, its respect for institutions, its pluralism, and in the scope it accords for individual energy to flourish. And it is compassionate both in the root sense of acknowledging our fellow-feeling with each other, and in drawing the circle of our moral concern around those with whom we are, and have been and will be, interdependent.

Equally, however, it belongs to neither the paternalist nor the libertarian traditions. It is closest to another tradition, the distinct and long-ignored "Old Whig" tradition, with its roots in Adam Smith and Edmund Burke, and its modern flourishing in Oakeshott and Friedrich Hayek. It is not paternalist, because it is realistic about the capacity of the state to improve our lives; and because it does not assume a relation of subservience between "we" and "they", between governed and governor. On the contrary, it is egalitarian. It sees our elected politicians as the Ancient Greeks saw them: as citizens first and foremost, in whom a temporary, limited and qualified trust has been placed to exercise public power on our behalf. And in keeping with its emphasis on conversation, this trust in turn implies mutual consideration and respect, and a pushing down of power and accountability away from the centre and towards the people.

Yet at the same time the new conservatism does not regard individuals as mere economic agents, or as composing groups or segments of society which must be successively wooed and bought off with favours from government. It is not the desiccated economic atomism of neoliberal economics, in which individuals are understood as isolated agents, cut off from others, or merely as economic automata. It insists not merely that we are all in this together, but that *all of* all of us is. A political viewpoint that ignores human dignity or energy or creativity in the name of *rigor mortis* economics impoverishes itself to that degree.

No. Present-day conservatives will be closer to Hayek when he said that the whole nature and character of individuals is determined by their existence in society. Markets are then seen for what they are: not as ends in themselves, but as limited and constrained means—albeit the greatest means yet devised—to generate wealth and prosperity, and to challenge bureaucratic authority.

But the deeper argument does not stop there, for even within the new conservatism there are at least three rather different strands of ideas now in play: we can call them the religious, the fraternal and the civil strands. Each has its own strengths and weaknesses. How they blend together will decisively affect the character of the Conservative party, and indeed that of the Coalition government.

The religious strand is grounded in Christian teaching, and naturally focuses on issues of social injustice, poverty, exploitation and deprivation. It is internationalist in its concern with human beings as such, as moral agents rather than as citizens of any particular country. To greater or lesser extent, it claims knowledge of some revealed truth about human nature, and its political authority rests upon this basis. The effects of this are to give it an explicitly moral—indeed moralistic—character.

The fraternal strand is grounded in philosophical reflection, and concerned with issues of social and personal well-being. It focuses on people as social beings, who find identity in relation to each other and thereby define the limits of their society, be it as club, tribe, village or nation state. It recognises the value of human institutions, their role in shaping their members and society more widely, and the degree to which these institutions stand as guarantors of stability between the individual and the state. Its political authority derives from shared experience and so from evidence, rather than revelation. Yet even within this strand there are distinct alternative threads: one more communitarian and social, the other more personal and individualist.

The civil strand is grounded in traditions of constitutionalism and statecraft. Its focus is on the conditions of human freedom, and its political authority that of custom, practice and precedent. It sees people not as moral agents nor as social beings, but as citizens subject to and equal before the law. It recognises Britain as the origin of the modern rule of law and the protection of individual rights. And it does not confuse the clear need to preserve our security in the face of global terrorism, with the ugly panoply of our wider surveillance culture.

These traditions overlap, but there are genuine differences of content and tone between them. The religious strand is wonderfully high-minded; but its emphasis on revelation and tendency to moralise make it unpersuasive to many people. It runs the risk of appearing to say, for example, that if tax policy favours married couples because marriage is a Good Thing, then the wife who divorces an abusive husband has done something wrong.

The fraternal strand has an attractive focus on the quality of human relationships, and on what it is to be human as such. But, at least in its communitarian version, its insistence that identity is a purely social matter constantly threatens to push it towards a utopian statism of its own. The civil strand is non-moralising and individualistic. But its world can seem airless, procedural—and in its insistence on preserving personal freedoms, both bad judgement and bad politics in an era of global terrorism.

Each of these traditions acts as inspiration in its own right and corrective to the others. Each brings something distinctive to the table—a central reason why recent debate on the political right about the nature of society and the proper remedy for social ills has been rather rich and interesting. Thus the religious viewpoint analyses social decline as a matter of loss of faith, of social authority and moral values; the fraternal viewpoint analyses it in terms of a decline in neighbourliness, in trust and in shared identity; the civil viewpoint in terms of growing state prerogatives and personal disempowerment. These views are not always consistent—consider, for example, the contentious question of whether the state should fund religious adoption agencies, on which the religious and civil strands have clearly different priorities. But they frequently support each other. It is precisely because of their disparate voices that each must play its part.

The same is true for what has become known as Red Toryism. This emphasises many of the themes outlined here, especially in its critique of state expansionism and neoliberal economics, which it expands into a trenchant attack on monopolies and a call for tougher competition policy. Its analysis of the erosion of working-class wealth is also important and timely. In so doing it pulls together elements of the religious, civil and fraternal strands described above, combining insights from catholic social teaching with an emphasis on the value of social networks and localism.

Compassionate Economics

Yet the new conservatism also includes a distinctively conservative economics, founded on the insight that the foundations of economic prosperity are social foundations: independent institutions, competition, and widespread entrepreneurship. There is a marked contrast between this dynamic and creative perspective and the static sterility of our orthodox economics.

Recall that as a political viewpoint, the new conservatism stresses independent institutions and horizontal human ties, the conversation of many equal voices over the command of one voice, the wisdom of crowds over the fallibility of central control. Its emphasis is not on what the state can do for you, or you for the state, but on what we can do for each other. It is a philosophically coherent and well-founded viewpoint, not merely an adventitious group of ideas or a laundry list of policies.

This Compassionate Economics reflects and extends these deeper commitments. In the first place, it rejects any monopoly of ideas—and so it has no truck with the present monopoly of textbook economics within British government. It opens the doors to new wisdom both within the discipline and outside, and it places a great responsibility on those in government to become wiser as to the limits of their thinking. We have seen a huge amount of recent interest in behavioural economics, through discussion of books such as *Nudge* and *Predictably Irrational*. Compassionate Economics consolidates and extends this line of thought, and blends it with insights from other more neglected areas of economics, and from other disciplines such as history and philosophy.

Secondly, Compassionate Economics does not privilege economics as such, but sees it as one language, one partial and limited way of representing the world, among many. It recognises what unreliable guides even the greatest economists may be when they cease to describe, and start to advise and predict. It understands that often the greatest power of a mathematical model is purely rhetorical: as a means to recruit others to a predetermined view. It rejects the increasingly accepted hierarchy in which economics trumps politics—as though the ability to point to a detailed cost-benefit analysis or statistical regression automatically exhausted political debate. It detests jargon and unwarranted deference. It is sceptical of consultants and advisers who enjoy many of the privileges of power without its responsibilities. It prefers open debate, plain words and common sense.

Thirdly, Compassionate Economics is generous in its view of people. It sees them not merely as economic agents, but as high-energy bundles of capability and potential. It rejects the idea that economics itself is a purely sterile and formal discipline. It seeks to break the loop in which government treats people like cattle, reinforces social demoralisation—and is then somehow surprised when people opt out or object. It is naturally predisposed to human freedom.

A Conservative Ethical Tradition?

Is there, then, a distinctively conservative ethical tradition? There is, and it starts with Aristotle's claim in the *Politics* that "man is a social animal". The word for "social" here is *politikos*, which also means "political". What Aristotle means is that mankind is part of nature, and man's own nature is to be with others, in a *polis* or city-state.

This remark may seem banal today, but in fact it is both a deep insight and a decisive intellectual break with the legacy of Plato. Recall that in Plato's famous image of the Cave, a few people are able to get away from looking at illusions to escape into the outside world, and supposedly to see Reality as it is. They have knowledge of the Forms, the universal ideas or principles that for Plato constitute reality, and that unite morality and the exact sciences. It is this knowledge that qualifies them to be political leaders, and that supposedly ensures that they will rule wisely.

Aristotle questions every aspect of this rationalist picture. He does so not merely as a philosopher but as a working scientist, indeed the most revered scientist in the ancient world. By locating man baldly within nature, he directs attention away from Platonic abstraction towards what is given, towards the here and now—and so towards a deeper understanding of humans as individuals and as a species. Knowledge is grounded, not in some mystical access to the idealised world of Forms, but in the study of the actual world as it is. The basic ethical question of how we are to live becomes rooted not in *a priori* reflection, but in an understanding of how we in fact do live.

As social animals, of course, humans grow up in society with each other. They learn to act well or badly, and so character is shaped by context and upbringing. Virtue is thus seen by Aristotle not as some Platonic will inspired by abstract moral universals, but as a disposition shaped by habit, culture and tradition. Change is understood as necessary, organic and gradual, not as innately desirable and disjointed from the past.

We can see the same tension in play at the dawn of the modern political era. Consider again Hobbes's famous social contract: a bargain whereby we give up some autonomy to a sovereign power which will maintain order and so protect us from our enemies domestic and foreign. This contract was not a historical event, and is nowhere written down. It is a game-theoretic abstraction from life. It thus falls squarely within the rationalist, Platonic tradition. And as Aristotle did with Plato, so Burke attacks this view at its deepest point.

For Burke, as for Aristotle, man is a social animal. There can thus be no explanatory value to considering a state of nature in which man is somehow to be understood independently of society: man's natural state is civil society itself. Where Hobbes deliberately ignores trust, culture and tradition, Burke treats them as constitutive of our human-ity. Where Hobbes stresses the primacy of the individual will, Burke stresses the natural reciprocity of rights and duty which occurs within society. Where Hobbes sees freedom as negative, lying in the absence of constraint, Burke lays the ground for freedom as a positive value, as a capacity afforded by society for an individual to flourish. For Burke it is in the very constraining institutions of an ordered society themselves, in the "little platoons", that freedom is to be found.

The 2009 Reith Lecturer Michael Sandel has been widely ac-claimed, especially on the political left, for his critique of market fundamentalism and his call for "a new morality of government and citizenship". But it is notable that Professor Sandel first made his name by advancing just the same underlying critique against John Rawls's famous theory of justice. Like Hobbes and Plato, Rawls invites us to enter a thought-experiment: to judge moral issues from behind a "veil of ignorance", in which we do not know in advance what role or status we will have. And like Burke and Aristotle, Sandel questions the starting assumption that pries a person away from society. We are, he insists, intrinsically social animals.

In his Reith Lectures, he extends this view still further. Questions of what we should do in society are unavoidably moral questions, he says. This moral aspect cannot be explained away, as economists and technocrats might desire. But equally, it cannot be reduced to a one-size-fits-all moral calculus. Each question must be analysed on a case-by-case basis. The right ethical approach engages with these difficult issues, but in a spirit of humility: aware of the possibility of failure, and full of respect for what is given in our culture, and for man's place in the world. It is a very Aristotelian picture. And a very conservative one.

Nowhere is this clearer than in the treatment of justice. A conservative will naturally feel a conflict of principles here, between respect for the rule of law, and the desire to ensure substantively just outcomes in specific cases. The result may be small acts of mercy, or widespread social reform. But a conservative will also instinctively avoid the grand but vague claims about social justice which have become so familiar in recent years, and which often yield social manipulation and undesired outcomes rather than justice itself. And it is noticeable that Professor Sandel adopts precisely this approach.

These Aristotelian and Platonic traditions continue to structure debates even today about conservatism as against liberalism and socialism. But the emphasis falls in a different place in each case. Socialism derives its utopianism and belief in the state ultimately from Plato—and the moral conflict between conservatism and socialism focuses today on the role of the state and its impact on human well-being.

But the philosophically deeper conflict is the one we have noted between conservatism and liberalism. For this is a conflict about the nature of human freedom: the precondition for choice, and so for morality itself. The liberal view is arid and technocratic—a game-theoretic view in which man is understood as pure will, and freedom as the absence of constraints on that will. Nothing could be further from the conservative's positive moral insistence on man as human animal and on human culture, institutions and capabilities.

Why, then, does all this matter? Why must a "new morality of government and citizenship" draw on this conservative ethics? A first answer is this: because that ethics is based on values such as respect for others and for tradition, aspiration, and personal freedom and responsibility—values which have been actively undermined in many ways by recent British government. Such an ethics goes with the grain of human nature. It is cautious, not sweeping; probing, not ideological. It does not make a fetish of ideology or theoretical consistency. Indeed, the thought that there can be no absolutely consistent worthwhile ethical theory is a conservative insight, which has eluded some of the greatest moral philosophers.

But another answer would be this: ignoring human beings and human nature is always disastrous for society. The greatest evils of the 20th century—think of Hitler, Stalin, Pol Pot and others—were committed by rationalist rulers in the grip of an extreme political or religious or racial theory about society and "the good". But Aristotle was right: men and women are social animals, with all the glorious variety, scope and imperfection which that suggests. They cannot be laid on some Procrustean bed of ideology.

And finally, these extremes apart, we can see the same phenomenon closer to home in our flawed public understanding of economics. And, yes, the intellectual foundations of this idea lie in liberal rationalism, as we have seen with the work of John Stuart Mill. The result of this thoughtless over-commitment to abstract theory by government and the banks has been economic catastrophe in our time. Thus the conservative ethical tradition described above is not merely of passing interest. It is fundamental to our moral, civic and economic renewal.

Left-Wing, Right-Wing or What?

Politically, what emerges is both new and distinctive. As we have noted, the present view rejects many of the policies and all of the basic approach to government of the last Labour government. Not merely as misguided, but as utterly misconceived.

But it also offers a clear critique of recent Conservative policies, and in particular of some of the keynote policies of the Thatcher government. To its huge credit, that government faced down and ultimately reversed decades of relative economic decline. But it also centralised large parts of our public services. In its zeal for reform, it sometimes regarded existing institutions simply as impediments to necessary change. And its focus on economic goals and improving people's material prosperity seemed to move public attention away from a richer sense of human purpose and human worth.

By contrast, the present viewpoint is less intellectually radical and more conservative. It is unabashedly pro-market, but sees markets differently to the present conventional view of them. It is neither controlling nor simply laissez-faire. Its emphasis on Institutions, Competition and Entrepreneurship is founded not on a purely economic conception of human good, or on "happiness", but on a profound and considered respect for individuals and for human capabilities. It is principled, but not rigidly so. Rather, it is pragmatic and non-ideological in character; a matter of instinct and judgement rather than the one-size-fits-all application of a political doctrine.

The effect of this is that, the new conservatism cannot easily be described with the established political categories of left and right. But this also gives it more freedom to innovate, sometimes very vigorously, and more freedom to act in accordance with simple common sense. Rules are necessary for effective government, but so are simplicity and a measure of discretion. Giving consumers more choice is often a good idea, but sometimes it can be a mistake. Private ownership is the heart of capitalism, but sometimes private companies are not the best means to deliver a public service. What results is a politics of doubt, not of faith—of judgement, not of ideology.

In part for this reason, the new conservatism seems to capture and unify many apparently disparate threads of thought now within the centre-right. It gives deep intellectual support to the critique of the state and instinct for pluralism, diversity and decentralisation. It explicitly embraces good public services, as a means to empower people, but implies a reshaping in the way those services are delivered. Indeed, it suggests that there are enormous gains in efficiency and the prevention of waste to be had from a more intelligent approach to delivering public services, as we will discuss below.

More positively, the emphasis on institutions accords very well with current concerns for the family. But it also fits well with the stress now being laid on strengthening the institutions of government, including a more powerful and independent-minded Parliament, and new measures to safeguard monetary and fiscal policy from overly political interference. And most importantly, it recognises that any worthwhile idea of social or personal responsibility requires us to see people as both capable and free, and to help them to be so. This is the common root of social and economic policy alike.

So far, then, we have a vision. The question now is how to translate it into a programme for government—into the Big Society. This is the subject of the next chapter.

11 **The Big Society**

You can call it liberalism. You can call it empowerment. You can call it freedom. You can call it responsibility. I call it the Big Society.
David Cameron

I am not a radical. I am a conservative who has been forced to become a radical.
Arnold Schoenberg

The Big Society is widely thought of as a political programme. But it is much more than that. It is a set of interlocking ideas, even a philosophy: a concerted and wide-ranging attempt to engage with the twin challenges of social and economic decline, and to move us towards a more connected society. It rests on a bold conjecture, that lying beneath the surface of British society today is a vast amount of latent and untapped potential energy. We have looked in detail at some of the constraints holding that energy back: state growth, centralisation and regulation; *rigor mortis* economics; and massive misunderstanding of human nature and human motivation. Behind these in turn lie the great giants of poverty, inequality, class division and lack of political imagination. They are the ultimate targets of the Big Society.

Releasing this energy is not a simple matter, especially since the Big Society fits into no ready-made political category. It is not just a matter of changing how things are, but how we think they are: of making British society a little prouder, more calm and self-confident, and more responsible. But we have seen similar bursts of energy in peacetime over long periods of British history in the 18th and 19th centuries. And there is evident scope for us to aim at this colossal prize with some confidence.

The Big Society as a Political Programme

Such a monumental shift in culture is not, then, a matter for government as such, but for us all. In the words of the columnist Matthew Parris:

> *Little by little, and like a virus, the Big Society idea has lodged itself insidiously in my mind; so that now, everywhere I go, I start to see small things that actually could be done closer to the ground, by and for the people who know about them and need them. And these small examples, most of them trivial in themselves, are beginning to add up to something that, incrementally, could make a big difference. There are so many, once you start looking.*

But as well as individual action, there is a clear role for public policy. What, then, can we expect from the Big Society as a political programme? Both in his original Hugo Young lecture and in a speech of July 2010 after becoming Prime Minister, David Cameron focused on several key themes. These included social action, public service reform and community empowerment, devolution of power to local government, and encouragement of co-operatives and mutuals. He emphasised the role of government not merely as channel of public funding, but as a promoter of greater transparency and provider of information to the public. Similar ideas have been developed by other senior political figures, including Iain Duncan Smith, Oliver Letwin, Francis Maude, Greg Clark, Nick Hurd and Nat Wei, all of whom have departmental or advisory responsibilities relating to the Big Society.

In a wide-ranging Cabinet Office presentation in July 2010, Lord Wei cast the Big Society as the culmination of a process of change in the public services that began with the origination and development of the Welfare State, a reining back of state provision after 1979, and increasing use of markets and active government policy after 1997—perhaps a rather kind way to describe the Blair-Brown period. Societies should be thought of as ecosystems, he said, operating on three levels: citizens and neighbourhood groups; social, private and state providers of public services; and government. None of these should predominate over the others. Greater involvement of people in their local communities would reduce isolation, strengthen social ties and increase self-reliance. It would build the capabilities of both individuals and institutions, and bring forward a new generation of citizen leaders. The result would be both a stronger society and better government.

Writing in 2006 in *Compassionate Conservatism*, I suggested that we might expect certain key policy planks from a new Conservative government, including

- *A large-scale programme of state decentralisation*: pushing more power and responsibility back to local councils and town halls, cutting back regional government, deregulating key markets such as housing, and introducing greater competition into the benefits system and the NHS, for example.

- *Much greater empowerment of intermediate institutions*: such as long-term plans and transition funding for universities that wish to become independent and offer needs-blind admission; locally elected police chiefs and opposition to the mergers of police forces; deregulation of the not-for-profit sector; and far more freedom and less bureaucracy for primary and secondary schools.

- *A greater emphasis on sharing British culture*: for example, through a voluntary programme of national public service aimed at old as well as young, through support for sport in and out of schools, and through policies that move away from the present multiculturalism that divides different ethnic and religious groups, and towards a greater civic awareness.

- *A celebration of individual freedom*: and so implacable opposition to ID cards, to DNA collection from the innocent, to a national identity register, and to the recent curtailment of freedom of speech; a drastic simplification of the tax system; and a drive to renew our rather seedy present political culture.

- *An Audit of Government*: asking every major government function, what its purpose and role is at present; what that purpose should be; and how best, if at all, it should be carried out in future. It is inevitable, and right, that such an audit will force us to reconsider the limits of personal and local responsibility. Should individuals bear personal responsibility if they are ill as a result of their own unhealthy lifestyles? Should families bear more responsibility for old age care? Should a given community bear more responsibility for law and order, for education or welfare? And to what degree should the costs of these choices be imposed on others?

So it has proved. It is notable how much early Coalition poli-cymaking has followed the broad guidelines of the Big Society. The flagship education legislation creating Free Schools has at its heart a deep belief in human capability and the importance of schools not simply as buildings but as independent institutions. Civil liberties have been enhanced with the scrapping of ID cards, the National Identity Register and ContactPoint, the centralised child database. Twelve pathfinder mutuals have been set up by which entrepreneurial public sector staff can run public services. Major new legislation to simplify benefits and reduce welfare dependency, to localise planning and empower local government, and to introduce National Citizens' Service is in preparation. The 2010 Spending Review has aspired to be as much a fundamental re-examination of the role and purpose of the state, as a recitation of specific spending priorities.

What is perhaps most striking is the apparent willingness of the Coalition to do what is normally regarded as politically unmention-able: give up power. There have been no great set-pieces like Gordon Brown's decision to make the Bank of England formally independent. But the early signs are unmistakeable. There is a greater sense of cabinet government. The Chancellor has given a veto power to Par-liament over appointment of the Head of the new Office of Budget Responsibility. Vast amounts of previously hidden local and central government spending data have been made public.

Of course, the proof of the pudding is in the eating. But already we can say this: the Big Society's political programme is being vigor-ously implemented. It is likely to amount to the most thoroughgoing attempt for a century to redefine the relationship between the indi-vidual, the state and public and private institutions. It is conservative in inspiration and radical in execution. Disraeli would be proud.

Addressing the Critics

But of course, the idea of a Big Society has hardly been uncontested. On the contrary, there has been sharp criticism from all parts of the political compass. We will look at these in ascending order of seriousness.

First comes the claim that the Big Society is empty, or incomprehensibly vague. This is just untrue. The idea is grounded in British thought, culture and practice, as we have seen. It is vague at the edges, as all political ideas are vague at the edges. But the core is coherent and intellectually substantive; and it carries with it both a persuasive diagnosis of the main causes of British social and economic decline, and a ruinous critique of the effects of Fabianism on the political left. Not only that: the idea indirectly highlights the pathology of government inherited from Gordon Brown. There is a huge misconception, especially in the media, that if an idea is not directly tied to some centrally-driven agenda, top-down intervention or state spending, then it has no substance. But a key part of the Big Society is precisely not to set a one-size-fits-all policy, but to encourage pluralism and diversity.

Second is the claim that the Big Society is poor politics for the Conservative party. This may or may not be true; but it is hardly a real criticism, since the overriding political question is never what is good for any party but what is good for the country. There is some evidence that the Big Society as a key political theme was introduced too late into the 2010 General Election campaign to have real impact with the electorate, and indeed it may even have confused voters. But that bears on the conduct of the campaign, not the idea.

Third is the suggestion that the Big Society is "really" about volunteering and philanthropy, or sponsorship of the arts or charities by the wealthy, or more specifically about the transfer of public services into the third sector. Of course volunteering, philanthropy, charitable giving, private sponsorship and social action all lie close to the heart of the Big Society. There is, moreover, much more to be done in each of these areas, as many people have noted. But it would be absurd to pretend that they are the whole of what is intended by it. The idea that public services could ever simply be transferred wholesale into the third sector is a hopeless canard, given the relatively small size of the latter. But it is equally clear that the third sector is the home of vast innovation and social energy, as is the private sector, and that these resources need to be more widely and intelligently deployed.

Fourth is a cluster of related and overlapping criticisms: that the Big Society is a con trick, or latter-day Thatcherism in disguise, whose purpose is to paper over a programme of privatisation and cuts to public spending motivated not by economic necessity but by Conservative ideology.

This is the core claim of present political opposition. It raises the interesting question why, if it is a con trick, so many people on the left should be keen the claim the idea as their own. But it should at once be clear that the Big Society is a coherent and logical expression of a conservative tradition which goes back to the 18th century; that this line of thought has been at the centre of the Conservative party's modern thinking ever since the election of David Cameron as leader in 2005, and arguably well before that; and that while it shares with Thatcherism a belief in the "vigorous virtues" of human beings, it is at sharp variance with both the libertarianism and the political centralisation of the 1980s. It is certainly not a con trick.

Nor is it "ideological". Of course the Big Society, like any political philosophy worthy of the name, has a line of argument within it. Indeed its argument is one that specifically recognises the over-extension of the state, and the dependency and inefficiency which that over-extension has caused. To that extent there are cuts to be made which are welcome, wise and long overdue. There are others which are the deeply regrettable results of over-spending by the Blair and Brown governments, and it is one of the tragedies of the current circumstances that some good people and great organisations will be affected by the overriding need for government to take control of the nation's finances and reduce the deficit. But the key point is that the argument is being made not in a fundamentalist spirit but thoughtfully, and with an openness to disagreement and contrary evidence. To repeat Michael Oakeshott's words, this is a politics not of faith, but of doubt.

The fifth and deepest potential criticism comes not from politics but academia, in the form of the widely celebrated book *The Spirit Level* by Richard Wilkinson and Kate Pickett. The book's central claim is that greater economic equality within a given society is associated with a vast range of improved social outcomes, covering crime, education, health and a host of other measures. It has been taken up enthusiastically by those on the left who believe that the analysis justifies much higher levels of taxation and redistribution of income, and an even greater degree of social engineering, than the UK has at present. These measures would be anathema to the Big Society.

In fact, however, *The Spirit Level*'s authors themselves wisely shy away from this conclusion, from an awareness that the paths into and out of economic inequality are extremely complex and vary massively across different societies. To give one example, between 1950 and the early 1990s the USA experienced huge economic growth, heavily fuelled by increases in personal consumption. Just the kind of circumstances in which die-hard critics of capitalism might expect rising inequality. Yet inequality in fact fell significantly over this period.

Economic equality is an important political value. But it is not the only one, and there is no royal road by which to reach it. Societies are all different from each other, and the authors are rightly sceptical of reductive economic policy prescriptions.

It may come as a shock, but the overall message of *The Spirit Level* is actually very supportive of the Big Society. Indeed some of its underlying themes are almost identical: that economic success is built on social foundations, for example, and that narrow economic or financial measures of well-being are unreliable, and perhaps even dangerous. Above all, in its wealth of comparisons between different countries the book brings out the obvious but fundamental point that even apparently similar societies can radically differ from each other. There is, in short, nothing pre-ordained about the way we live now. *It doesn't have to be this way—we could be doing much better.*

As such *The Spirit Level's* true target is in fact the current Labour party. For under its Fabian influence, the party has come to associate all positive social change with increases in state spending. Three further things have then quickly followed. The first is a tendency to identify state and society, ignore the myriad ways in which they are at odds, and assume that all public services must be state-owned and state-funded. The second is a tendency to believe that the main measure of a society's well-being lies not in relative outputs (how well it is doing) but in relative inputs (how much is being spent). The third is a tendency to think that all reductions in state spending are automatically suspect, no matter how wasteful, bureaucratic or constraining they may be. Behind them is a bleak belief that there is no alternative, and that those advocating other positive change are at best wrong-headed and at worst immoral. To all of these views *The Spirit Level* is a salutary corrective.

The Counterfactual Case

Finally, we need to address the So What? criticism. Would a Big Society approach, with its emphasis on I-C-E—institutions, competition and entrepreneurship—really have made any difference during the recent horrendous financial crisis and economic recession?

The answer is Yes. We can say with certainty that it would have helped. It might even have allowed us to escape the crisis, as some other countries did. Recall that according to the old textbooks, the financial crash of 2008 should never have occurred at all. Aware of the potential risks, people would supposedly not have borrowed so much, banks would not have lent so much, the regulatory system would have been barely tested and the interbank and money markets would have continued to function without government support. Yet that colossal crash did in fact take place, markets seized up, many famous banks ceased to exist, the powers of government to manage economic disorder were stretched to breaking point, and the human consequences have been and will continue to be dire. No greater proof is needed of the limits of man's economic rationality.

From a policy perspective, the crash revealed a gigantic failure of governance: within financial institutions, within the regulators and within government itself. When it came, the crash was unlike anything seen in Britain since the 1930s. It was triggered by a collapse in asset values rather than a decline in profitability as such; a set of circumstances for which regulators were unprepared and lacking in the appropriate corrective mechanisms. But the seeds of British vulnerability were sown much earlier, as we have seen. The banks competed furiously with each other to grow their mortgage books with poorer and poorer credits. The Government took the badly motivated and foolish decision in 1997 to remove banking supervision from the Bank of England, an issue over which then-Governor Eddie George almost resigned. There was a huge consequent loss of supervisory experience and expertise, and a damaging dispersion of regulatory responsibility under the so-called tripartite system. Both the Government and the regulators were far too complacent over the course of a decade in the face of escalating warning signs, in a sector that still over-dominates the British economy. The Government itself hugely over-borrowed at the top of the market. And the lack of cash savings as people borrowed to invest in property made them doubly vulnerable to recession, and continues to depress economic recovery.

So what difference would an I-C-E perspective have made? In the first place, it would have made all involved—politicians, regulators and bank executives—far more aware of how hard humans find it to assess risk, and of the well-known human predilection to prefer a benefit now, and to discount or ignore future costs. Secondly, it would not have allowed those politicians, regulators and executives automatically to assume that markets can efficiently assess the creditworthiness either of individuals or banks. Thirdly, it would have been clear from the outset as to the importance of the Bank of England standing as lender of last resort, a role which is inexplicable on the standard economic model, in which prices are always efficient and liquidations are already priced in and so do not affect markets. And fourthly, it would have had a far more realistic conception of the importance of competition within financial services: as a means to greater efficiency and better allocation of resources, and not simply as a good in itself. The result would have been a far more sceptical and realistic attitude to the various booms already described.

Above all, I-C-E would have made us all far more sensitive to the dangers posed by the changing nature and increasing size of financial institutions. The old financial order had many weaknesses, but crucially, its institutions had clearly defined roles. The commercial banks and building societies had capital from depositors and investors, but took as little risk as possible. The brokers and merchant bankers were advisers and agents. They acted on behalf of investors and corporate borrowers, who took the risk and made the returns or losses.

The beauty of the whole lay in the different and interlocking roles of the various players, and the minimisation of conflicts of interest. And this was helped by the different institutional forms involved. The banks were companies, because they needed shareholder capital to sustain their balance sheets. The building societies were mutuals, because the mutual form facilitated the extension of credit to the less well-off. The brokers and merchant bankers were partnerships, because they did not need much capital and knew that their partners would guard their own funds far more zealously than those of any outside shareholders.

But look now at the financial markets, and what do we see? The original roles of these institutions have been submerged in a huge wave of capital. Conflicts of interest have become massive and endemic. Partnerships have disbanded. Building societies have demutualised. And thus the pluralism and diversity of their institutional forms have been replaced by one monopoly form: that of the shareholder corporation. Our financial markets have been damagingly corporatised.

With this corporatisation has come three things. First, there has been a deep and damaging separation of risk and reward. When the markets go up, the banks do well. When they go down, the shareholders—and ultimately British taxpayers—suffer. Secondly, there are now no natural limitations on the size of financial institutions. As the fallout of the Lehman Brothers bankruptcy showed, an increasingly large number of financial institutions cannot be allowed by government to fail—yet it is barely within the power of government to save them. And thirdly, the financial services sector has increasingly been seen simply as an industry like any other, rather than as providing the fundamental plumbing on which the global economy relies.

Any worthwhile solution to these problems will stress the role of institutions, competition and entrepreneurship. But the Big Society also has deep implications for other areas of reform, as we shall see.

12 What's Next?

> The power of jazz is that a group of people can come together and create art, improvised art, and can negotiate their agendas with each other ... and that negotiation *is* the art.
>
> **Wynton Marsalis**

So what's next? Where is the Big Society headed? What else should a reforming government focus on? What should WE do to support social and economic reform?

These issues are so large that they far outstrip the scope of this short book. However, rather than run the whole gamut of policy now, let's look at three radically different areas where a Big Society approach could directly improve our future well-being: in social reform, in economic reform and in public service reform. In each case, the new perspective opens up new ideas and new opportunities. We will come back to finance and economics later in the chapter. But we start, perhaps surprisingly, with music.

The Social Power of Music

We have already seen the profound difference which a focus on human capability would make in secondary education. But now think what it would mean to import a capability agenda fully into policy on the arts, culture and sports. These areas have long been treated as lesser priorities by government, although the National Lottery has in many ways been a brilliant institutional innovation. But a government that saw human capability at the heart of social and economic regeneration would surely place huge emphasis here.

To take just one example, we need to move music, musical performance and singing from the political periphery to a central role as a social and economic, as well as cultural, priority. The research evidence now clearly shows that music confers huge social, cognitive, emotional and therapeutic benefits, especially on those who take an active part in it. These benefits have been demonstrated for specific groups such as prisoners, neonates and children, or those with mental or physical disabilities or dementia. But they are not confined to those groups; on the contrary, they are open to us all, and they have already been widely recognised in other countries across the world from Venezuela, with its famous "El Sistema", to Cuba to Finland.

Thus music has highly beneficial neurological effects; for example, singing together releases oxytocin, a neurochemical which appears to increase feelings of trust between people. It aids brain development, and encourages creative thinking and problem-solving. It teaches people to work better in teams, through bands, orchestras and choirs. It imposes a need for individual self-discipline and practice. It promotes a sense of mutual respect and aspiration to reach the highest standards. It gives priceless insights into other cultures and other ways of thinking, yet demands reflection on its own history and development. It is open to all, and no respecter of persons. It can be intensely competitive, or highly co-operative. It can flourish at any level, from the simplest nursery rhyme through a twelve-bar blues to the subtlety of a raga and the staggering virtuosity of a Paganini or Liszt. But it never, at any level, loses its essential connection with the human emotions, or with emotional truth.

British music education has had a long and often distinguished history. After 1950 a nationwide network of local music services was set up to provide instrumental and singing teaching, instruments and sheet music. Local authorities were required to fund their music services, which worked within primary and secondary schools. In addition, there were local bands and orchestras, which fed competitively into county youth orchestras. Thus the way was fairly open for young people from all backgrounds to learn an instrument and progress up a ladder of achievement. In a few cases this might culminate in a music college and professional career. In many more the result would be great learning and joy. But for all involved, musical performance would be something they owned and felt part of. Each music service was, it has been said, a mini-sistema in its own right.

Today, however, much of the music education in this country is a mess. There have been valuable government initiatives under Labour, such as the Music Standards Fund and the Sing Up! choral project in primary schools. But millions of young people, especially from the poorest and most disadvantaged families, have had limited access to or enjoyment of playing music. Meanwhile a series of futile culture wars have been played out in which music, and specifically classical music, has been depicted as an elitist activity only open to the wealthy few, rather than a massively empowering activity for the many. Anti-elitists might care to recall that Joseph Haydn grew up in a desperately poor rural Austrian household and was expelled from school for misbehaviour; Louis Armstrong grew up in and around Storyville, the New

Orleans red light district, and learned to play the cornet at a home for delinquent boys.

These culture wars have been buttressed by a mythology of talent and "genius" which suggests that only a few people have the requisite ability to play; when in fact the truth is that almost everyone has musical ability, but that hard work and focused practice are what really matter. Within music education itself there has been a long and unhelpful stand-off between advocates of classical music and others who are equally passionate about world music, jazz and other forms. There remain 157 music services across the country, but they are struggling to make ends meet as these and other factors undermine popular understanding of and belief in music.

The contrast with sport is telling. Over the years different governments have rightly recognised the cultural and social importance of sport. It has seemed obvious to ministers that sport elicits huge popular passion, promotes high standards and excellence, confers great physical benefits for those who take part, and can help us to engender a happier and more inclusive society. Exactly the same is true of music, and more. Yet political interest in the social power of music has been apathetic.

The Coalition government has made an excellent start in this area, with the Department for Education ordering a new review of music provision, despite huge financial constraints. But this is only the start of a long journey, and Conservatives should lead the way. For it was in fact a Conservative government which released local authorities from the statutory requirement to fund county music services after 1988, an important reason for their decline.

What is to be done? Three things: first, start talking at all levels about the importance of music; look at the evidence; study what is being done in other countries; and use this information to shape public opinion and interest in music. Secondly, invest in teacher training, and extend the highly innovative TeachFirst programme to include music teaching. Thirdly, renew the statutory obligation on local authorities to fund their music services after 2012-13, and support these local authority commitments with new funding to help music services invest in new choirs and orchestras, and to extend their services to musical opportunities for adults. Yes, this involves a spending commitment. But the numbers are far less than might be imagined: £5-£6 per pupil per year, or say £60-£80 million a year to cover all primary and secondary schools, plus orchestras. That's a very modest amount; roughly half the average *daily* interest payment on our current fiscal deficit.

Local government has become enmeshed in unfunded statutory obligations and "guidance", as we have seen. This is one area in which a funded obligation is justified. Music is universal to all human culture. It knows no barriers of class or income. Like the arts and education generally, it is one of the marks of a civilised society. It must be so for the Big Society.

Reforming Corporate Governance

From music to business. We have already seen how financial institutions have increasingly become shareholder corporations. Perhaps this should not be surprising, for the corporation or company is by far the most influential economic institution in the world today. Well over 90% of all non-governmental economic activity is conducted through corporations. Our media are saturated with the brands, imagery and values of corporations. We live in a world of corporate capitalism. And these corporations are not functioning as well as they should do. Many companies, and many banks, are not being run fully in the interests of their shareholders.

The issue is not so much that of corporate responsibility, important though that is. It is one of ownership and accountability. Pooling resources in corporate form allows people to do more and to share risk. Corporations were originally enabled by specific grant of the sovereign to encourage risk-taking and the creation of capital. And in due course they came to enjoy limited legal liability. Why? Because it was widely recognised that corporate activity served the public good, and it was widely believed that corporate power would be limited to actions consistent with the public good. Thus a whole nation could benefit from the fruits of exploration, innovation and trade.

But today many of our largest public companies resemble bad governments in their levels of risk aversion and bureaucracy. They may have the outward forms of good governance. But the reality is that their managements are often complacent and unaccountable, while auditors, remuneration consultants and corporate pension fund trustees are insufficiently independent. These firms are too focused on the short-term, and too much of their revenue is used up in executive compensation. Twenty years ago the average chief executive of a FTSE 100 company earned 17 times the average employee's pay; now it is more than 75 times.

We have had many useful reports and governance codes over the years. But the real point is that there is still a huge vacuum of ownership. These firms have investors who regard investments as betting slips, not owners who regard them as property. All parties have in effect swallowed the standard economic view, in which managers and directors are merely agents of the shareholders, corporations are merely bundles of contractual relationships, and there is no sense apart from the effects of the invisible hand in which corporations exist to serve the public good.

And they have used that view to rationalise inactivity, by pointing out that there is often a "free rider" problem in which an active owner bears 100% of the costs but only part of the benefits of their ownership. And so corporate value is lost, often until the point where the company is bought by venture capital funds with a small number of very active owners who can then take the steps necessary to rebuild it.

But here again the standard view is both partial and inaccurate. The directors of a corporation are legal fiduciaries, not merely economic agents. The shareholders are owners, not merely investors. The original institutional context, which linked appropriate corporate power to public wellbeing, is largely missing. The result is to destroy value and entrench underachievement.

This is not a rant against Anglo-American capitalism or the need to reward talented people: quite the opposite. But the evidence across the UK and US is pretty clear. Many reputable studies have been carried out looking for a significant and sustained correlation between senior executive compensation and long-term corporate performance: none has been found. Instead, there is a close correlation between executive pay and size of company, creating a strong incentive towards increased takeover and merger activity. Takeovers always benefit senior managements, win or lose. But in fact 60% of them destroy economic value. This is a direct result of current compensation arrangements.

By contrast, well-owned companies deliver better long-term performance, and are recognised as doing so. A 2002 McKinsey study which looked at 200 top global investors found that three-quarters of them would pay a premium for companies with good governance. Two other studies, from ISS and Deutsche Bank, have found that good governance improves profitability and lessens risk in US and UK companies respectively.

What, then, can government do? The key is to promote the exercise of independent ownership: by institutional shareholders, by corporate directors, and by trustees in corporate pension funds. Here are four simple suggestions for how to do so. The first is for government vigorously to enforce the trust law of ownership on companies and financial institutions. A share's vote is part of its value, and the trustees or directors of these organisations should be made clearly legally accountable for its proper exercise. The second is to make it easier for shareholders to nominate entirely independent non-executive directors of their own choosing to corporate boards, perhaps by cumulative voting. The third is for non-executive directors alone to choose remuneration consultants and auditors, via the relevant board committees. And the fourth is for pension fund trustees, many of who are also corporate employees, to be explicitly required to act solely in the long-term interests of their beneficiaries, and to be protected in law when they do so.

These are four simple ideas, in the unsexiest of policy areas. But their effect is potentially enormous. Making more companies work slightly harder through better ownership would have a gigantic effect on Britain's competitiveness and prosperity as a nation. It would lift profitability, employment and pay scales, while restraining remuneration in the boardroom. And even a small improvement in shareholder returns would massively strengthen the country's pension system over the long term.

Restoring the Human Touch to Public Services

Over the past 50 years government has tried many different structures and approaches to the provision of the public services, repeatedly confronting the basic truth that state control tends to inefficiency while completely free markets can lead to unfair outcomes.

Earlier we noted how conventional economic thinking had reinforced a tendency in government to centralisation and top-down control of people through the tax and benefits system. That thinking ignored independent institutions, in both the private and third sectors. And it wrongly treated people as economically rational in the standard neoclassical sense. On the one hand, they were expected to be able to understand and cope with the fantastic complexities of the tax credits system, of pension credits and other benefits. On the other, these systems ignored the systematic ways in which people do in fact misjudge risk, assess uncertainty and deal with loss.

Again, a Big Society approach would imply a significant reshaping of public services to reflect how people actually think and behave. It would mean a systematic focus on empowering front-line staff and allowing them to get on with the job—giving them the ability to gain the autonomy, mastery and purpose that we have seen are the sources of creative motivation. It would mean taking many of the least well-off people out of the tax system altogether, as the Coalition has done, rather than submit them to the complexities and unanticipated losses of the Tax Credits system. In a similar vein, in future it would mean a reduction in pensions means-testing and a huge simplification of Pension Credits. And it would mean a careful extension into other areas of health and social care of Direct Payments and Individual Budgets, which allow many disabled people more autonomy and control over their lives.

But there is a much bigger prize still to play for. This lies in the way the state interacts with people. As we have seen, at present the state uses an operational model for delivery of public services which is based on a Theory X view of management and so generates an obsession with cost and cost-control. It attempts to depersonalise, segment and proceduralise all interactions with individual people; it fragments personal responsibility and accountability; and it insists on expensive and cumbersome processes of verification and audit. The apparently paradoxical results are huge unexpected costs and waste, employee demoralisation and poorer outcomes.

This is, again, not a small topic for discussion. But the direction of reform should be clear. What is needed is to move towards seeing each strand of public service as a distinct institution, and specifically a complex system, in and of itself; to relax the present obsession with cost control in favour of a focus on quality; and to treat users and employees not merely as economically rational agents but as human beings.

Here's the difference. At present the public services divide users into standard and unusual or problem cases. The standard cases go through the system according to a set of pre-set rules. The problem cases are identified at various points and are then shunted off to special units specifically tasked with sorting them out. The idea is that by enforcing this separation the bulk of cases can be dealt with at the lowest level of cost, by staff who require very little specific training or expertise. More highly trained staff are used on the problem cases.

All perfectly sensible, one might think. But one would be wrong. The effect of separating out the problem cases is to relieve any pressure on the organisation as a whole to understand them, or improve the overall treatment of its users. It tends to create public services that, despite the best intentions of those who set them up and those who run and work in them, are often far too tolerant of failure. This lowers unit costs in some areas. But it increases the overall cost of the organization because it generates huge "failure demand"—the costs and stresses required to fix something which has already gone wrong.

The result is that the state spends ever more just to stay in the same place. The public become deeply frustrated and angry with "the system" of public services, and apathetic about politics. And centralisation, paperwork and delay are further increased. After all, what can you expect if the only way a citizen can get a proper human response to her concern is by writing to the MP, who in turn forwards the correspondence directly to a Minister?

But if you look at any successful organisation, from Google to Toyota to Innocent Drinks, they are characterised by a relentless focus on improving the user's experience. Happy users ask very little of the organisations that serve them, so that "failure demand" is kept to a minimum. The effect is that a focus on quality does not increase, but in fact minimises, long-run costs. Why should the British public sector be any different?

A Culture of Long Termism

So far we have looked at different kinds of reform. But the Big Society is not just about making existing institutions work better; it is also about creating good new institutions. One new institution which would offer enormous public benefit to us would be a British sovereign wealth fund.

Recall that in textbook economics income and wealth are treated as equivalent. A stream of annual payments can be discounted back to a given lump sum amount, and the standard theory implies that we should be indifferent between the two. But applied to policy, this idea embodies a crucial and highly convenient fallacy. For it can be true—and it is often in fact true—both that the stream of payments and the lump sum are mathematically equivalent, and that they are radically different in their political and policy implications. A government oriented to national wealth will seek to protect and enhance its capital, and invest it in capital assets. An expenditure-oriented government will feel freer to use its capital for current spending. It will also feel freer to take on capital obligations today in the belief that these are simply streams of future expenditure whose funding later governments can be left to wrestle with.

Governments like to spend without taxing, and they like to promise capital sums without the unpleasant necessity of having to pay for them immediately. Over the past 30 years they have regularly felt free to do both. Under the Thatcher government, the proceeds of North Sea oil and of privatisation were largely incorporated into current spending. The same has happened under Blair and Brown, and to these proceeds have memorably been added much of the country's gold reserves and the £22 billion-plus receipts from the auction of 3G mobile telephone licences in 2001. On the other side of the public balance sheet, since 1997 there has been a huge build-up in liabilities, notably for public pensions, over and apart from the debt incurred from the financial crisis. It is no coincidence that there has also been a significant loss of interest in party politics among young people, who increasingly believe that the baby boomers have hijacked the Exchequer.

The Norwegians, however, have taken a different approach to their wealth, more in tune with I-C-E and the Big Society. In 1997 they established the Government Pension FundGlobal, as a continuation of the Government Petroleum Fund set up in 1990. The initial capitalisation was NKr 48 billion. In every year since then the national accounts have shown a capital surplus, of which between 60% and 99%

has been transferred to the fund. The fund has also grown through its own active and diversified financial management.

As a result, the Norwegians now have a sovereign wealth fund with a value of NKr 2.8 trillion, roughly equivalent to £300 billion today. It is controlled by the Norwegian Ministry of Finance, run by the national bank in four offices worldwide through expert independent money managers, and it is formally accountable to the Norwegian parliament. It is inexpensively managed. Its accounts are a model of jargon-free public explanation and transparency.

The fund has three functions. First, it manages the public oil and gas revenues of the country, as a capital resource for the benefit of future generations. Secondly, it manages the national bank's foreign exchange reserves. Thirdly, it manages a petroleum insurance fund, as a reserve to cover losses and liability arising from Norway's investments in oil and gas.

Norway is thus a huge worldwide equity investor. Unlike some purely financial investors it takes its ownership rights extremely seriously, following guidelines mandated by the Norwegian parliament. As a result, the fund increasingly holds companies in which it is invested directly accountable for their actions—in line with our emphasis above on improving corporate performance—and it publicly lists and will not invest in those that do not measure up. Such companies currently include Raytheon, Thales and Lockheed Martin (cluster munitions), Serco (involvement in nuclear weapons), Wal-Mart (breaches of human rights) and Freeport McMoRan (environmental damage). The US firm Kerr-McGee has been listed but subsequently readmitted.

The Norwegian approach has much to recommend it. It is successful, long-term, transparent, ethical and democratic. It gives Norway huge clout in the global capital markets, which it can and does use to encourage best practice. And it gives the Norwegian people a clear understanding of their national wealth and of the endowment that this generation will pass on to its successors, and so on. Nor does the fund constrain the powers of parliament. Parliament can change the formal purposes of the fund, or even dissolve it. The Ministry of Finance can transfer as much capital surplus as it chooses, when it chooses. The government can ultimately spend the capital assets just as it wishes, or has been democratically mandated to do.

So the real issue here is not economic, but political and moral. It is a matter of what constraints government should be under to account for its actions. Current spending of capital receipts is a free ride for politicians, in which they can costlessly mortgage the prospects of the next generation to satisfy the present one, or their own pet projects. This should not be so. One function of a UK sovereign wealth fund would be to build proper transparency and debate into a crucial aspect of UK economic policy.

A sovereign wealth fund of this kind does not fetter government. But it makes it more accountable. A finance minister who wishes to sell the country's gold reserves cannot simply act alone, but must (quickly and discreetly) make the argument—and be judged publicly on the consequences. A prime minister who wishes to contract new public sector pension liabilities must explain how these stack up against the assets held in the fund, whether or not these have been pledged to public pensions. After a huge windfall such as that from 3G mobile licence sales, there would be immediate pressure to add the new funds to the national asset fund.

Over the years we have learned to be nervous about political interference in monetary policy. We have learned the value of new institutions such as the Lottery, which manage public resources semi-independently of government. So also now with national wealth. And there is always the economic benefit to be considered. The accountants PWC once estimated that if the UK had invested its North Sea oil receipts in a sovereign wealth fund, the fund in 2008 would be worth £450 billion. That is the same as total UK tax revenues for 2007-8. Add in the £70 billion or so of UK privatisation proceeds, plus 3G mobile receipts and accumulated interest, and you would have well over £600 billion. Even outside the fund, the British economy would be stronger, since it would not have been artificially sustained by these enormous unearned capital flows over 30 years.

The UK is heavily in debt at present, so setting up a sovereign wealth fund might seem premature. In fact, however, the exact opposite is true. First, the goal that it addresses, of ensuring greater fiscal transparency and accountability in British government, is an absolutely vital one. The value of such a fund lies not merely in the pool of wealth which it creates, but in the institution, and in the example of disciplined and accountable economic management, which it establishes. We need a new fiscal settlement in this country. New institutional means are required to create the necessary accountability, and this is one important move towards that goal.

And there is a more specific reason. The British government now owns the Northern Rock bank. It has just been forced to take significant, not to say controlling, stakes in Royal Bank of Scotland, Lloyds TSB and HBOS. Nominally, the government has little direct influence over the operations of these institutions. In reality, politicians, interest groups and the media have tried to exert huge pressure for the government to push these institutions to make more politically helpful decisions over repossessions, credit and internal rationalisation. But while there needs to be a thorough overhaul of banking regulation, it is of vital importance to insulate the banking system from too much political interference during this process. What better way to launch a new sovereign wealth fund than by committing these assets into it, and ensuring the transparency and accountability that the system so conspicuously lacks at present?

The Rediscovery of Politics

These are just a few policy ideas. But what they point to is more profound: the rediscovery of politics. As we have seen, we have been enslaved by three pernicious and mistaken ideas: that politics is only about the relationship between the state and the individual; that individuals are fundamentally economic automata; and that any derogation from perfect competition is a cause of inefficiency and makes some people worse off. The result is to drive both political and economic debate into a dead end.

Ultimately, breaking free from these mistakes requires the thought and energy of all. It is not enough for a few key people at the top to change their minds. It will not be achieved purely by the recent change of political or administrative personnel within No. 10 Downing Street. On the contrary, if it is to be effective it requires a gigantic transformation in the beliefs and expectations of our public administration. The shift in institutional perspective must be very widely shared within government—including parliament, agencies, quangos and local government—and it must reflect a distinct, well-articulated and shared public conception of the new approach.

Much of what is needed will focus on the detailed machinery of government, and includes such things as a thorough revamping of standard manuals, documents and procedures within the Civil Service; retraining of public officials, both those in technical positions and their "clients"; properly cautious and independent briefings for ministers on the likely effects of key decisions; and strengthening of the capabilities of select committees. Some of these moves are already under way.

But it also implies a different attitude on the part of our politicians. One of the lessons of the past ten years has been to remind us of the dangers of over-reliance on a certain kind of officially certified expertise. External consultants have proliferated. In many cases their supposed professional expertise does not actually embody genuine understanding. But even where it does, professional advisers are often far too uncritically used, to avoid responsibility rather than to inform decision-making. And the overall effect is to suggest that many genuinely political matters are in some sense "merely technical": to substitute economics for politics, and to relegate politics to the margin.

But this reflects a profound misunderstanding. Politics is quintessentially, and in the best sense, an amateur activity. Not necessarily amateurish, of course: it can always be carried on in a professional and competent way. But of its nature, it involves endless trade-offs between incommensurable priorities and values. Do you build this airport, or save this wilderness? Do you create these new hospitals, or put extra money into child support? Do you increase the state pension, or spend more on the armed forces and anti-terrorism measures? As soon as politicians adopt a particular professional viewpoint—be it that of the businessman, the environmentalist, the doctor, the social worker, the soldier, or the economist—it becomes more difficult for them to strike the right balance. Expertise can only get you so far. More valuable by far are experience, wisdom, independent judgement—and common sense.

Among other things, then, the Big Society allows us to rediscover what we already know. It gives a measure of common sense—about people, about institutions, about markets, and about what government can do—back to British political debate. It highlights the limits of each mode of thought: economic, political, administrative, scientific, legal. It sets the scene for the revival of ideas that have been driven to the sidelines by our financially dominated culture—ideas of public duty, vocation and honour, and of civic pride. It reminds us of what this country historically stood for in the world: a beacon of tolerance, civility, enterprise and personal freedom under law. It puts new and forgotten possibilities back into play, and encourages us to ask what kind of politics, and what kind of economy, we want. *It doesn't have to be this way; we could be doing so much better.*

By challenging the present cosy assumptions within our politics and public administration, it clears the way for new ideas, new energy and new creativity. Government is constrained and held properly accountable. New institutions and new voices are made possible. The people are empowered, they know more, and they prosper.

Afterword: **A Few Radical Thoughts**

> The country needs—the country demands—bold, persistent experimentation. Take a method and try it. If it fails, admit it frankly and try another. But above all, try something.
> *Franklin Delano Roosevelt*

We need not seek to emulate FDR's hyperactivity. But what follows are a few final and perhaps more radical suggestions for economic and financial policy, made from the perspective of the Big Society. They remind us that a deeply conservative viewpoint can have rather unconventional implications.

Restrain Excessive Pay

Bashing financiers and big business has become very cheap politics; and Conservatives in particular are rightly squeamish about attempts by the state to set pay levels and to intervene in private contracts. But even so there is legitimate public concern about levels of pay within companies and financial institutions, which have been driven upwards in part by *rigor mortis* economics. After all, the commercial banks in particular have always been semi-public institutions; and what matters is entrepreneurship and wealth creation, not rewards to corporate size or executive status.

There is now a lot of evidence to suggest that bonus deals pushed the banks to take excessive positions in the markets, increased systemic risk and fuelled the financial crash. Moreover, very high compensation appears to draw off able people from other areas where their social and economic contributions would be greater, and in particular from entrepreneurial businesses. Finally, while very high bonuses seem to work well as incentives to perform routine work, we have seen that the evidence is that they undermine—that is, actually reduce the level of—people's performance in creative activities.

This creates what we might call the Paradox of Creativity. We often hear how creative certain financial or business activities are, and how this supposedly warrants very high pay in order to attract talent. But the truth seems to be that the more creative the activity, the *less* those involved should be remunerated by very high bonuses.

Direct government intervention via pay caps is ill-conceived and likely to be self-defeating. But here are a few other suggestions. Increase the disclosure of senior executive pay. Ensure that as a matter of course it is staggered across several years, escrowed and released against actual performance. Pay those working in banks not in shares, but in subordinated debt to ensure their focus on the financial stability of the balance sheet. De-link fees for head-hunters and compensation consultants from executive compensation. Finally, encourage firms—and indeed quangoes and government bodies—to market senior jobs very publicly at the *lowest* level of pay benchmarked for the position, not the highest. After all, such jobs rarely lack suitable candidates, and they carry considerable prestige.

Tougher Competition Policy

Competition is one of the crucial determinants of economic success, as we have seen. It should follow, therefore, that competition policy is a matter of great public interest. In fact, however, it has become lost in lengthy and technical legal disputes, often dominated by international law.

However, on a Big Society approach government would not rest comfortably on the legal arcana of anti-trust, state aid, market liberalisation or merger policy. On the contrary: it would be more actively monitoring the profitability of different sectors of the economy, and supporting infrastructure development, deregulation and other measures to stoke competition and increase market access for new companies. This is well understood in the case of overseas markets, such as in agriculture. But it also applies to UK markets. A case in point is again the banking sector, where there is a strong case for more competition in both wholesale and retail banking.

The argument is often made that very high levels of profitability should be ignored given the public interest in the taxes received. This neglects the point that such profits often reflect an uncompetitive transfer of wealth from individuals or corporate clients, who would themselves pay additional tax if able to retain the cash as profit.

Needed: a Rebate on the Private Finance Initiative

At a time when the public sector is under huge pressure, the private finance initiative offers substantial untapped savings for the Exchequer. Legally, the PFI sits in public-private limbo. It is not part of the public sector, since its consortia are made up of private contractors. But nor is it entirely in the private sector, as these same consortia manage hundreds of public projects, from roads to schools and hospitals.

These projects are paid for by the Exchequer on 25- or 30-year contracts, with contractors typically aiming at 8-10 per cent annual returns; a healthy taxpayer-guaranteed return, especially in a very serious recession. Given this, contractors should be asked to contribute a rebate to the public purse, by reducing the interest payments they receive from public institutions. Some £210bn of PFI capital assets remain outstanding. A McKinsey study last year suggested that a reduction in interest charges paid to contractors by NHS hospitals of just 0.02 or 0.03 per cent could save £200m. (The NHS constitutes about one-third of the PFI debt.) Taken across all existing contracts even this modest rebate could save £500m.

These savings would not go to the Treasury, but would be remitted back to each of the relevant projects, typically hospitals or schools. They would give a pound-for-pound support to the funding of each institution, from the bottom up; in other words, a lot more medicine, surgery and school books.

It is true that these are private companies with commercial contracts signed with willing counterparties; and it should be no part of government policy to seek to tear up these contracts. But we are in a financial crisis, and there is a clear inequity in the additional pain that will be felt by non-PFI organisations from fiscal consolidation, while their PFI counterparts remain commercially sacrosanct.

The government does not lack the influence to encourage PFI providers to rebate a portion of their revenue. Indeed, there is a direct precedent for exactly this sort of rebate in the so-called "voluntary code". The code was agreed in 2002 after several PFI providers made huge windfalls refinancing deals. Under it, 30 per cent of gains from existing projects were returned to the taxpayer. The ratio is 50 per cent for new deals. PFI consortia have played a part in rebuilding Britain's infrastructure. Now they must play their part in rebuilding that nation's finances too.

A Leaner State

The final point is perhaps a slightly unexpected one. As we have seen, the emphasis of the Big Society falls on society, on improving public services, and on releasing social energy.

We have, moreover, seen some of the unhappy social and economic effects of our recent over-reliance on the state. But the counterpart of this is, as we have seen, to make the state better at what it does do: leaner, stronger and more resilient in responding to shocks.

First, it must not be forgotten that in the recent financial crisis it was the nation state—and specifically the state's ability to tax, fund and regulate the financial system in a crisis—that provided the final if imperfect backstop. Much deeper thought is still needed as to specific mechanisms by which future financial crises can be avoided or mitigated. After all, nearly every aspect of the existing safeguards regime has been found to be wanting—early warning system, monitoring of financial liabilities, regulatory regime, capital adequacy, crisis procedures, international co-ordination.

Secondly, as a nation we face huge future deficits in the funding of pensions and adult social care, which will worsen as the baby boomers continue to retire and longevity increases. The state is the only remotely plausible means at present to address the deep issues of intergenerational equity and social insurance raised by these challenges.

Thirdly, the growing influence of corporate power relative to the nation state, and what President Eisenhower once called the military-industrial complex, require both a doctrine of countervailing national power, and the provision of effective collective legal remedies to uphold the public interest.

Fourthly, "the state" does not just mean central government. Local government is older in origin, and exercises more direct influence over people's lives. It needs to regain a far higher measure of financial and operating autonomy, and must not be ignored as the Big Society seeks to localise services and push power down into communities.

Finally, the ultimate test of the Big Society will lie in whether it can genuinely rebuild our economy and revive our society. But for those who still doubt its meaning, or who fear it means public services on the cheap, the real political test lies in our future prosperity, not our present adversity; not in how much money is saved during the current fiscal consolidation, but in how and where the new government chooses to spend and invest, at a time when more people than ever rely on good public services. That spending and those investments, be they in a new benefits system, revitalized education or a nationwide superfast broadband network, will reveal the long-term character, aspirations—and indeed capability—of what already promises to be a great and reforming government.

Acknowledgements

This book is the final result of a five-year project whose goal has been to set out a coherent intellectual and practical basis for the New Conservatism. It recapitulates and extends the argument of my previous pamphlets *Compassionate Conservatism* (Policy Exchange, 2006; with Janan Ganesh) and *Compassionate Economics* (Policy Exchange, 2008). However, it also draws extensively on *From Here to Fraternity* (CentreForum, 2007) and *Churchill's Legacy* (Liberty, 2009; with Peter Oborne), as well as various other pieces of journalism mentioned in the Endnotes. I am very grateful to my co-authors, and to these organisations, for their support.

Many of those who helped with those pamphlets also influenced this book, and I thank them again. In particular I should like to thank Lee Auspitz, Oliver Hartwich, Robert AG Monks, Torquil Norman and Casey Norman. Jonathon Flegg was very helpful in finding and sourcing new research. Christopher Woodhead and his colleagues at the University of Buckingham Press have handled the manuscript with typical efficiency and despatch.

I am also grateful for their comments, ideas or support to John Adams, Tim Besley, Phillip Blond, Nicholas Boles, Chris Cook, Greg Clark, Matt Hancock, Rupert Harrison, Tom Hirons, Alan Hodson, Terence Kealey, Danny Kruger, Andrew Laird, Oliver Letwin, Tim de Lisle, Tim Montgomerie, Charles Moore, James O'Shaughnessy, Matt

Ridley, Iain Duncan Smith, Andrew Sullivan, Nat Wei and several academic readers who have preferred to remain anonymous. Needless to say, none is responsible for errors in what remains.

I remain more indebted than I can say to my beloved wife Kate Bingham, and to our children Sam, Nell and Noah Norman.

Endnotes

In the text we deliberately use some shortcuts for reasons of simplicity or readability. Thus we use "conventional economics", "textbook economics", "economism", "*rigor mortis* economics" and the like more or less interchangeably. The same is true for "the UK" and "GB". However, we distinguish between big-C "Conservatives", who are affiliated to that party; and "conservatives", who may in principle belong to any political party, or to none. Classic works of economics or philosophy are not cited.

Introduction

Cameron on the Big Society: Hugo Young Memorial lecture, 10 November 2009; see also his Liverpool speech of 19 July 2010

Archbishop of Canterbury: quoted from remarks at a Lambeth charity debate, 23 July 2010

Freedland articles: "A two-faced coalition is hard to fight but Labour needs to find a way, quick", *The Guardian*, 13 July 2010; "There's a good idea in Cameron's 'big society' screaming to get out", *The Guardian*, 20 July 2010

Big Society literature: see e.g. *Small State, Big Society*, Localis, 2010; *Growing the Big Society*, IPPR, 2010; *Civic Streets: the Big Society in Action*, Demos, 2010; *Connected Communities: How social networks power and sustain the Big Society*, RSA, 2010; Paul Ormerod, *N Squared: Public Policy and the Power of Networks*, RSA

Planet 1945: Simon Jenkins, "As Cameron gets radical, the left dozes on planet 1945", *The Guardian*, 10 August 2010

Recent books supporting themes in *Compassionate Conservatism* and *Compassionate Economics*: George Akerlof and Robert Shiller, *Animal Spirits*, Princeton University Press, 2009; Roger Bootle, *The Trouble with Markets*, Nicholas Brealey Publishing, 2009; Nicholas Christakis and James Fowler, *Connected*, Little Brown, 2009; Daniel Pink, *Drive*, Canongate, 2010; John Quiggin, *Zombie Economics*, Princeton University Press, 2010; Yves Smith, *Econned*, Palgrave Macmillan, 2010; David Orrell, *Economyths*, Icon Books, 2010; Phillip Blond, *Red Tory*, Faber and Faber, 2010

Chapter 1: The British Economy: Miracle or Mirage?

Inequality: Jesse Norman, "Inequality: Labour's shame", *The Guardian*, 25 February 2009

Relative real GDP growth: *National Accounts of OECD Countries*, OECD

Population growth since 1992: *Population Trends*, Office of National Statistics

Rise in house prices: *Nationwide House Price Index*, Nationwide, April 2008

Current savings rate: *Office of National Statistics*, June 2008

Equity withdrawal: *Housing Equity Withdrawal*, Bank of England

Public spending and waste: David Craig, *Squandered*, Constable, 2008

Immigration: *The Economic Impact of Immigration*, House of Lords, April 2008

NHS productivity: "Take Your Pick", *Economist*, 4 March 2006

OECD study: *Programme for International Student Assessment* (PISA), 2006

Chapter 2: The State We're Really In

Thatcher government and the state: Simon Jenkins, *Accountable to None*, Hamish Hamilton 1995; *Thatcher and Sons*, Allen Lane, 2006

State share of GDP: HM Treasury

State employment: Fraser Nelson, *Spectator*, 25 February 2006

Faking civil society: Dave Clements, "Faking Civil Society" in Dave Clements, Alastair Donald, Martin Earnshaw and Austin Williams, *The Future of Community*, Pluto Press 2008.

Giddens: Anthony Giddens, *The Third Way*, Polity Press, 1998

Changing nature of government and its corruptions: see Peter Oborne and Simon Walters, *Alastair Campbell*, Aurum Press 2004

Negative impact of public spending on GDP growth: David B. Smith, *Living with Leviathan*, IEA, 2006, Ch. 3

Productivity: Pre-Budget Report speech 1997, Pre-Budget Report 1998

Government productivity report: *Sunday Times*, April 2004

NHS inflation: *NHS 2010: Reform or Bust*, Reform 2005

NHS productivity: "Take Your Pick", *The Economist*, 4 March 2006

2008 fall in productivity under Gordon Brown: David Brindle, "Sharp fall in public service productivity", *The Guardian*, 27 July 2010

Baumol's Cost Disease: William J. Baumol and William G. Bowen, *Performing Arts: The Economic Dilemma*, Twentieth Century Fund, 1966. For more recent empirical support across a variety of sectors see "Baumol's Diseases: A Macroeconomic Perspective", William D. Nordhaus, *NBER Working Paper* 12218, May 2006

Chapter 3: A Fracture in Society

Social decline: for detailed analysis of these issues see the work of Iain Duncan-Smith and the Centre for Social Justice; in particular *Breakdown Britain* (2006) and *Breakthrough Britain* (2007)

Drug use: *European Monitoring Centre for Drugs and Drug Addiction, Annual Report*, 2005

Binge drinking: Institute of Alcohol Studies *"Binge Drinking" Fact Sheet*, 2006

Teenage births: *Innocenti Report Card*, UNICEF Innocenti Centre, July 2001

UNICEF report: *Childhood in Industrialised Countries*, UNICEF, February 2007

NEETs: *The Cost of Exclusion: Counting the Cost of Youth Disadvantage in the UK*, Prince's Trust and RBS, April 2007

Position of young people: Ed Howker and Shiv Malik, *Jilted Generation*, Icon Books, 2010

Voting patterns: *Power to the People*, The POWER Inquiry, February 2006

Green Book: HM Treasury, *The Green Book: Appraisal and Evaluation in Central Government*

Tax credits: House of Commons Public Accounts Committee, *Tax Credits and PAYE Eighth Report*, 2008

Single parents claiming tax credits: Frank Field, "Blame faulty tax credits for bad behaviour", *Daily Telegraph*, 3 October 2007

Excesses of consumerism: see e.g. Benjamin Barber, *Consumed*, Norton, 2007

Clone Towns: *Clone Town Britain*, New Economics Foundation, 2005

Smith on sympathy: Adam Smith, *Theory of the Moral Sentiments*, Edinburgh, 1759

Mill on economics: "On the Definition of Political Economy", in *Essays on Some Unsettled Questions of Political Economy*, 1964

Samuelson: Paul Samuelson and William Nordhaus, *Economics*, McGraw-Hill, 2004

Public Choice theory: James Buchanan and Gordon Tullock, *The Calculus of Consent*, University of Michigan Press 1962; see also Gordon Tullock, *The Vote Motive*, IEA 1976/2006

Kahneman and Tversky: see e.g. Daniel Kahneman, Paul Slovic and Amos Tversky, *Judgement Under Uncertainty*, Cambridge University Press, 1982; and Daniel Kahneman and Amos Tversky, *Choices, Values and Frames*, Cambridge University Press, 2000

Gary Becker: see e.g. *The Economics of Discrimination*, University of Chicago Press, 1957/1971

George Akerlof: see e.g. "The Market for 'Lemons': Quality Uncertainty and the Market Mechanism", *Quarterly Journal of Economics*, August 1970

Chapter 4: Rigor Mortis Economics

Inefficient markets: see e.g. Andrei Shleifer, *Inefficient Markets*, Oxford University Press, 2000; John Kay, *The Truth About Markets*, Allen Lane, 2003 and references; Bootle, op. cit.; Roman Frydman and Michael Goldberg, *Imperfect Knowledge Economics*, Princeton University Press, 2007

Welfare and imperfect information: see Joseph Stiglitz, *Whither Socialism?*, MIT Press, 1994

Behavioural economics: see e.g. the Kahneman/Tversky collections above; Richard Thaler and Cass Sunstein, *Nudge*, Yale University Press, 2008; and Nick

Wilkinson, *An Introduction to Behavioral Economics*, Palgrave Macmillan, 2008; also *The Impact of Price Frames on Consumer Decision-Making*, Office of Fair Trading, 2010

Operational models: see John Seddon, *Systems Thinking in the Public Sector*, Triarchy Press, 2008; also Chris Dillow, *The End of Politics*, Harriman House, 2007

Willingness to pay, and risk: John Adams, Risk, UCL Press, 1995

CCTV cameras: McCahill, M. and Norris, C. (2003), 'Estimating the extent, sophistication and legality of CCTV in London', in M. Gill (ed.) *CCTV*, Perpetuity Press. Cited in *A Report on the Surveillance Society For the Information Commissioner* by the Surveillance Studies Network, September 2006

Chapter 5: Left and Right

Keynes: quoted in David Marquand, *The Progressive Dilemma*, Weidenfeld and Nicolson 1999

Art of politics and art of government: the phrase comes from Ross McKibbin, "Good for Business", *London Review of Books*, 25 February 2010

Post-democratic politics: Colin Crouch, *Post-Democracy*, Polity Press, 2004; Peter Oborne, *The Rise of Political Lying*, The Free Press, 2005

Fabianism: there is a huge literature on this, but see e.g. M. J. Daunton, "Payment and Participation: Welfare and State-Formation in Britain 1900-1951", *Past and Present* 150, 1996; Mark Bevir, "Sydney Webb: Utilitarianism, Positivism and Social Democracy", *Journal of Modern History* 74, 2002

Purnell on sects: James Purnell, "Labour became too much of a sect", *The Guardian*, 19 July 2009

Labour's need for change: see interview with John Denham, *Fabian Review*, Summer 2010

Trotsky: see Jesse Norman, "Conservatism can save the left", *The Guardian*, 24 July 2009

Disraeli: see e.g. P. Smith, *Disraelian Conservatism and Social Reform*, Routledge & Kegan Paul, 1967

Tory statecraft: J. Bulpitt, "The Discipline of the New Democracy: Mrs Thatcher's Domestic Statecraft", *Political Studies*, 34/1, 1986

Rival traditions: W. H. Greenleaf, *The British Political Tradition*, Vol. 2, *The Ideological Heritage*, pp. 189-358, 1983

Chapter 6: The Foundations of Society

Hobbes: *Leviathan*, ed. Macpherson, Penguin1981

Absolute sovereignty: a fuller treatment would also focus on Locke, who anticipates some of our later discussion with his emphasis on the boundaries of sovereignty, on limited government and on individual rights

Civil and enterprise association: see Michael Oakeshott, *On Human Conduct*, Clarendon Press, 1975; *The Achievement of Michael Oakeshott*, ed. Jesse Norman, Duckworth 1992; and J. L. Auspitz, "Individuality, Civility, and Theory: The Philosophical Imagination of Michael Oakeshott," *Political Theory*, 1976

Oakeshott on rationalism and conversation: Michael Oakeshott, *Rationalism in Politics*, 2nd ed., Liberty Fund, 1991

Modes of experience: Michael Oakeshott, *Experience and its Modes*, Cambridge University Press, 1933

Politics of faith: Michael Oakeshott, *The Politics of Faith and the Politics of Scepticism*, ed. Timothy Fuller, Yale University Press, 1996. See also Andrew Sullivan, *The Conservative Soul*, Harper Collins, 2006

Philic association: to adapt Aristotle's terms, we can thus contrast philic (connected) association with nomic (law-based, i.e. civil) association and telic (goal-based, i.e. enterprise) association

Burke on the little platoons: Edmund Burke, *Reflections on the Revolution in France*, 1790, Liberty Fund, 1999; see also David Willetts, *Modern Conservatism*, Penguin 1992

Intermediating institutions: a fuller discussion here would include early 19th Century ideas in France on "intermediary institutions", and the views of Montesquieu, Constant and de Tocqueville

Friendship: see the third essay in Andrew Sullivan, *Love Undetectable: Notes on Friendship, Sex, and Survival*, Knopf 1998

Friendly societies; Peter Gray, "A Brief History of Friendly Societies", Association of Friendly Societies

Hayek on individuals: *Individualism and Economic Order*, University of Chicago Press 1948

Wise crowds: James Surowiecki, *The Wisdom of Crowds*, Abacus, 2005

Pericles: Thucydides, *The Peloponnesian War*, ii.65

Chapter 7: The Danger of Happiness

Theory X and Theory Y: see Douglas McGregor, *The Human Side of Enterprise*, McGraw-Hill, 1960/2006. Quoted in Seddon 2008

Affluenza: Oliver James, *Affluenza*, Vermillion Books, 2007

Spirit Level: Richard Wilkinson and Kate Pickett, *The Spirit Level*, Allen Lane, 2009

Layard: Richard Layard, Happiness: *Lessons from a New Science*, Allen Lane, 2005

Sen on capability: see Amartya Sen, "Capability and Wellbeing" and the other papers in Amartya Sen and Martha Nussbaum (eds.), *The Quality of Life*, Oxford University Press, 1993

Recent work on incentives: see Daniel Pink, op. cit. and works cited there

Free and open source programmers: Karim Lakhani and Robert Wolf, "Why Hackers Do What They Do: Understanding Motivation and Effort in Free/Open Source Software Projects", in J. Feller, B. Fitzgerald, S. Hussam and K.R. Lakhani, *Perspectives on Free and Open Source Software*, MIT Press 2005

Motivating scientists: Pierre Azoulay, Joshua Graff Zivin and Gustavo Manso, "Incentives and Creativity: Evidence from the Academic Life Sciences", *NBER Working Paper No. 15466*, National Bureau of Economic Research, 2009

Neuroscience of compassion: see in particular the work of Jean Decety and collaborators, via http://home.uchicago.edu/~decety/jean_ cv.html. E.g. "A Social-Neuroscience Perspective on Empathy", *Current Directions in Psychological Science*, 15.2

"Battery" children: C. Norton, "After a century, we've produced the stressed-out cooped up battery children of today", *The Independent*, 2 September 1999

High trust/low trust environments: D. Knoch et al., "Diminishing reciprocal fairness by disrupting the right prefrontal cortex", *Science* 314, 2006

Volunteering: *The Health Benefits of Volunteering: A Review of Recent Re- search*, Corporation for National and Community Service, 2007; also e.g. Allan Luks and

Peggy Payne, *The Healing Power of Doing Good*, iUniverse.com, 2001

Effects of diminished life expectancy on behaviour: Mairi Macleod "Die Young, Live Fast: The Evolution of an Underclass", *New Scientist*, 14 July 2010

Ofsted report on maths: *Mathematics: Understanding the Score*, Ofsted, September 2008

OECD school hours: *Education at a Glance 2008: OECD Indicators*, OECD, September 2008

For a fascinating and deeply supportive insight into how to enthuse young boys about reading and writing, see Gareth Malone, "Extraordinary school for boys: helping boys love literacy", *Daily Telegraph*, 2 September 2010

Chapter 8: Law, Liberty and Personal Freedoms

Entry powers and Harriet the cow: see Harry Snook, Crossing the Threshold, Centre for Policy Studies, 2007

Burke: op. cit.

Development of the common law: see J.H. Baker, *An Introduction to British Legal History*, Oxford University Press, 2002

Blackstone: Sir William Blackstone, *Commentaries on the Laws of England, 1765-9*, Standard Publications, 2007

Dicey: A.V. Dicey, *Introduction to the Study of the Law of the Constitution*, 8th ed., Liberty Fund, 1982

Rule of law: Tom Bingham, *The Rule of Law*, Allen Lane, 2010; Ferdinand Mount, *The British Constitution Now*, Heinemann, 1992

Parliamentary sovereignty: in general, see Jeffrey Goldsworthy, *The Sovereignty of Parliament*, OUP 1999

Chapter 9: Institutions, Competition and Entrepreneurship

Impact of William III: Douglass North and Barry Weingast, "Constitutions and Commitment: the Evolution of Institutions Governing Public Choice in Seventeenth Century England", *Journal of Economic History* 49.4, 1989; see also Tim Harford, *The Logic of Life*, Little Brown, 2008; and Harry Bingham, *This Little Britain*, Fourth Estate, 2007

Institutions: see also Tim Besley, *Principled Agents? The Political Economy of Good Government*, OUP, 2006

Entrepreneurship: see e.g. Israel Kirzner, *Competition and Entrepreneurship*, University of Chicago Press, 1973; and Jesus Huerta de Soto, *The Austrian School*, Edward Elgar, 2008

Co-ops: see Jesse Norman, "Buy into Cameron's Co-op", *Sunday Times*, 11 November 2007; Larry Elliott, "Co-operatives offer template for David Cameron's big society", *The Guardian*, 2 August 2010

Chapter 10: The New Conservatism

Bush's compassionate conservatism: Marvin Olasky, *Compassionate Conservatism: What it is, What it Does, and How it Can Transform America*, Simon and Schuster, 2000; also Tim Montgomerie, *Whatever Happened to Compassionate Conservatism?*, Centre for Social Justice, 2004

Communitarians: see e.g. Robert Putnam, *Bowling Alone*, Simon and Schuster, 2001; Amitai Etzioni, *The Common Good*, Polity Press, 2004

Red Toryism: Phillip Blond, op. cit.

Reith lectures: Michael Sandel, *Reith Lectures*, BBC, 2009; see also his *Justice: What's the Right Thing to Do?*, Allen Lane 2009

Conservative ethics: see Jesse Norman, *Citizen Ethics in a Time of Crisis*, Barrow Cadbury Trust et al., February 2010

Chapter 11: The Big Society

Matthew Parris: "I have finally seen how the Big Society might work", *The Spectator*, 5 August 2010

Lord Wei: *Building the Big Society*, Institute for Government, 6 June 2010

Claiming the Big Society for the left: e.g. Jonathan Freedland, "There's a good idea in Cameron's 'big society' screaming to get out", *The Guardian*, 20 July 2010; Anthony Painter, The 'big society': it's a funny thing but Cameron's on to something", *The Guardian*, 3 August 2010; Alastair Reid, "Let the Enemy In", *New Statesman*, 13 September 2010; Richard Darlington, "Don't Cede the Ground", *Progress*, 13 September 2010; Diane Abbott, "Labour's Family Roots", *Compass*, 21 September 2010;

Chapter 12: What's Next?

History of UK music education: Gordon Cox, *Living Music in Schools*, Ashgate Publishing 2002

Effects of music: Daniel Levitin, *The World in Six Songs*, Aurum Press, 2009

The primacy of work over talent: Malcolm Gladwell, *Outliers*, Allen Lane 2008; Geoff Colvin, *Talent is Overrated*, Nicholas Brealey Publishing 2008

CEO compensation: Polly Toynbee and David Walker, *Unjust Rewards*, Granta Books, 2008

Importance of owners: the modern literature on this is enormous, but see e.g. Robert Monks and Allen Sykes, *Capitalism without Owners Will Fail*, CSFI, November 2002; Robert Monks, *Corpocracy*, John Wiley 2007

Directors as fiduciaries, not agents: Robert C. Clark, "Agency Costs vs. Fiduciary Duties", in John Pratt and Richard Zeckhauser (eds.) *Principals and Agents*, Harvard Business School Press, 1985

McKinsey study: "A New Era in Governance", *McKinsey Quarterly* 2, 2004

ISS study: Lawrence Brown and Marcus Caylor, *The Correlation between Corporate Governance and Company Performance*, Institutional Shareholder Services, 2004

Deutsche Bank study: *Beyond the Numbers: Corporate Governance in the UK*, Deutsche Bank, February 2004

Public service: see Seddon, op. cit.

Norwegian sovereign wealth fund: see the Norges Bank Investment Management Annual Reports

Afterword: A Few Radical Thoughts

Pay: see Walker and Toynbee, op. cit; and especially David Bolchover, *Pay Check: Are Top Earners Really Worth It?*, Coptic Publishing, 2010

Bonus and PRP incentives: see literature cited in Chapter 9

PFI rebate: see also Jesse Norman, "Hard Times Call for a PFI Rebate", *Financial Times*, 16 August 2010

About the Author

Jesse Norman is one of the intellectual architects of the new conservatism. He is the MP for Hereford and South Herefordshire, Chair of the All-Party Parliamentary Group on Employee Ownership and a member of the Treasury Select Committee. Prior to entering politics he taught and did research in philosophy at University College London, was a Director at Barclays, and ran an educational charity in Eastern Europe during and after the Communist period.

A lifelong volunteer, Jesse sits on the boards of several charitable organisations, including the Roundhouse and the Hay Festival. He writes regularly in the national press. His books include *The Achievement of Michael Oakeshott* (Duckworth, 1992); pamphlets include *Compassionate Conservatism* (2006, with Janan Ganesh) and *Compassionate Economics* (2008), both published by Policy Exchange, where he remains a Senior Fellow; and *Churchill's Legacy* (Liberty, 2009, with Peter Oborne).

www.jesse4hereford.com